TOP GAMERS

6 Bajan

46 Captian Sparkles

60 Stampylonghead

30 StacyPlays

54 Dan TDM

16 CupQuake

100 TOP GAMING MOMENTS

8

The most iconic gaming moments of all time - how many have you seen?

TOP 100 GAME-CHANGERS

18

Discover the 100 top titles that changed the world of gaming!

38

HOTTEST GAMES
Discover some of the best games you should be playing right now!

BLOCK IN A POT!
Grow a Minecraft grass block today!

48

inside

PROFILE

Bajan Canadian

Real Name: Mitch Hughes
Channel: .youtube.com/user/TheBajanCanadian
Famous for... His Hunger Games Minecraft videos and songs.

⦿ INSTAGRAM

Apparently this guy gave Mitch lessons on how to play pool!

Bajan loves playing League Of Angels on his phone when not Minecrafting.

Mitch hanging out with a kangaroo pal on a trip to sunny Australia!

FAVOURITE GAME

Minecraft
Specifically, taking people down in the Hunger Games mod and testing out combat mods!

VITAL STATS

Channel start date:
3 March 2010
Subscriber count:
5,582,248
Most watched video:
Hunger Games Song

HEY DOOD!

1 **Pokemon Card Prank**
Mitch completely covers his friend's room in Pokemon cards while he's away – his reaction is great!

2 **Who's Your Daddy?! - Secret Cannon Blows Up Baby**
In this mini-game Bajan has to stop his friend from hurting himself – but it all goes horribly, horribly wrong.

OUR FAVE

3 **Bajan Canadian Song**
The Hunger Games song is really cool, but we love the one about himself and his adventures even more.

100 BEST GAMING MOMENTS

Call yourself a gamer? How many of these legendary 100 gaming moments have you experienced?

100
THE SIMS
(2000, EA, PC)

We all did it. Whether it was making them wet themselves or trapping them in a pool until they drowned, everybody tortured their sims and secretly liked it.

LIMBO

99
LIMBO
(2010, MICROSOFT, 360)

Giant arachnid versus defenceless boy: it's a mismatched fight that makes for an enthralling hunt to the death.

98
ULTIMA ONLINE
(1997, EA, PC)

The killing of the 'unkillable' Lord British – in reality creator Richard Garriott – during the game's Beta showcased the fallibility of developers and proved we gamers had real power.

97
MARIO & SONIC AT THE OLYMPIC GAMES
(2007, SEGA, WII)

Mortal enemies for so long, the eventual pairing of Mario and Sonic granted millions of wishes wished back in the '90s.

96
ZERO WING
(1991, TOAPLAN, MEGA DRIVE)

Toaplan's dodgy translation of Japanese side scrolling shmup-fest became an internet phenomenon, almost reaching the dizzy heights of popular memes Keyboard Cat and Dramatic Chipmunk. For great justice!

95
ADVENTURE
(1979, ATARI, ATARI 2600)

When Atari launched Adventure they somehow neglected to give any credit to the game's authors. But designer Robinett managed to smuggle a hidden message into the game, which not only secretly hinted at his input into its creation, but also ended up being the first ever Easter egg.

ZERO WING

ADVENTURE

JOURNEY

94
ANIMAL CROSSING
(2001, NINTENDO, GAMECUBE)
In Japanese folklore the Kappa is a green, dish-headed, river-dwelling creature, responsible for the drowning of horses. In Animal Crossing Kapp'n rebuffs the myths with some memorably amusing sea shanties about cucumbers.

93
WOLFENSTEIN 3D
(1992, ID SOFTWARE, PC)
The game that started the first-person shooter genre. It was the grandad to Doom, Quake and every other FPS.

92
SUPER MARIO BROS.
(1985, NINTENDO, NES)
You'd think after the first couple of bridge-based losses, Bowser would have chosen a less precarious spot on which to battle the world's favourite plumber.

91
MASS EFFECT 2
(2010, BIOWARE, 360)
The Normandy explodes
Having your main character die at the beginning of one of the most anticipated sequels of modern times was brave. Discharging him/her in a fiery sphere of Reaper-induced explosion was outright shocking.

90
JOURNEY
(2012, SONY, PS3)
At the end of a giant sand dune-slide, Journey's camera shifts to the side and we're shown the most beautiful sunset imaginable. After this highest of highs, the game drops you in a cold, gloomy pit. Weird.

89
ASSASSIN'S CREED REVELATIONS
(2011, UBISOFT MONTREAL, 360)
Hitman extraordinaire Ezio was one of modern gaming's great characters. We've watched this Italian's eventful life play out in front of our eyes and joypads, but even heroes don't live forever. So it was at the end of Revelations, as an old man passes away peacefully in a hidden crypt.

88
TOMB RAIDER
(1996, EIDOS, PLAYSTATION)
Gamers of a certain age will remember this one with a lump in their throats and a shiver down their spine. Lara slowly made her way through the brooding Lost Valley picking off raptors with her pistols, then the ground began to shake, the dramatic music flared... then... then... ARGH, RUN AWAY! Good times.

87
SUPER BOMBERMAN
(1993, HUDSON SOFT, SNES)
Not a game mechanic as such, but absolutely unmissable when you're playing with pals. A bomb here, a bomb there, a neat bit of manoeuvring to lure an opponent to his doom... or should that be BOOM!?

86
THE LEGEND OF ZELDA: MAJORA'S MASK
(2000, NINTENDO, N64)
It's never a good sign when the moon looks as if it's going to tumble down onto your bonces, but that's the dilemma facing the citizens of Clock Town. Link's got three in-game days to save them. Fail to master time travel and watch what happens!

85
ZELDA II: THE ADVENTURES OF LINK
(1987, NINTENDO, NES)
Evil doppelgängers are old hat in videogames nowadays (the Zelda series is obsessed with them!), but it was Shadow Link's '87 debut, as final boss no less, that heralded their popularity. This chap's obsession with jumping into 'good' Link's pointy master sword proved his eventual downfall.

84
BANJO-KAZOOIE
(1998, RARE, N64)
Back in '98, Mario and Banjo really were showing all other platformers how things were done. This particularly iconic - and festive - stage featured awesome sled races, a giant Crimbo tree and, erm... being turned into a walrus.

83
MEGA MAN 2
(1988, CAPCOM, NES)
Mega Man always been H-A-R-D, but Wiley's lair, the final stage of the pad-snappingly tough sequel, had even the series hardcore wailing like babies. How d'ya like them one-hit kills, eh? Lovely music, too.

82
SUPER MARIO BROS 3
(1988, NINTENDO, NES)
It may have been surpassed - in both fashion and practicality stakes - by Mario World, but the possibilities that opened up once Mario collected his first suit took series fans' collective breath away. To the skies, our portly plumber!

81
RED DEAD REDEMPTION
(2010, ROCKSTAR, PS3)
The iconic image of the desperado hero holed up, Butch Cassidy and Sundance-style, fighting wave after wave of baddies in a valiant but futile last stand... it was a Western idea even Rockstar couldn't resist. Marston may have met his maker, but his legacy - and his Redemption - lived on through son Jack.

80
METROID PRIME
(2002, NINTENDO, GAMECUBE)
Prime was an astonishing first-person reimagining of a classic side-scroller, but even after travelling across areas like the Chozo Ruins and Magmoor Caverns, nothing prepared us for the bleak, windswept barrens of Phenandra. When Samsus's visor iced-over, we shivered with her.

79
THE ELDER SCROLLS V: SKYRIM
(2011, BETHESDA, PC)
We've scaled some pernicious peaks in videogames - we even climbed the Tower of Babel in Xenogears - but for sheer, lovely wondrousness Skyrim's trek to visit High Hrothgar and to converse with dragon-dude Paarthurnax... well, it signalled a new high mark in game environments.

78
KIRBY'S ADVENTURE
(1993, NINTENDO, GB)
Reappropriate powers from downed baddies by... er, storing them in your gob. Kirby changed from mild-mannered ball to pulsating, fire-spewing ball of PAIN... wahey!

77
OSU! TATAKAE! OUENDAN
(2005, INIS, DS)
A giant meteor speeds murderously towards earth, threatening all of humanity. What to do?! Get our best scientists beavering away on a giant laser? Or save the day using... the power of dance? Get to it, Elite Beat Agents...

RED DEAD REDEMPTION

100 BEST GAMING MOMENTS

FAR CRY

76
METAL GEAR SOLID 4: GUNS OF THE PATRIOTS
(2008, KONAMI, PS3)

The legendary scene of Solid's first PlayStation outing gets a wonderful cameo in our old soldier's final adventure. Here both retro sound effects and even an inspired flashback that plays out in the original, now-ancient looking engine! Neat touch.

75
GUITAR HERO II
(2006, ACTIVISION, PS2)

Jacksonville Southern rockers Lynyrd Skynyrd's second most celebrated song - after Sweet Home Alabama, of course - features the greatest guitar solo of all time. Latter GH entries never got close to this nine-minute monster of an encore.

74
DOUBLE DRAGON
(1987, TAITO, ARCADE)

Billy and Jimmy Lee kung-fu kick their way through side-scrolling beat 'em up hell to rescue their maid Marian - but just who's girlfriend is she? The result: surprise sibling vs sibling boss super scrap!

73
WII SPORTS
(2006, NINTENDO, WII)

The first astonishing game started the motion control avalanche that led to games of Skyward Sword's calibre. And they're just getting started...

72
ETERNAL DARKNESS: SANITY'S REQUIEM
(2002, Nintendo, GameCube)

Look after your sanity meter or prepare for hallucinations, skewed cameras, fake technical issues and your head falling off. Silicon Knights never topped this.

71
SUPER MARIO BROS
(1985, Nintendo, NES)

The original and best? Well, we're not sure we'd spend too much time playing it now, but it's a solid gold classic.

70
SUPER METROID
(1994, NINTENDO, SNES)

Only seconds to get off an exploding base? But the game only started not five minutes ago! Better run...

69
CASTLEVANIA: SYMPHONY OF THE NIGHT
(1997, KONAMI, PLAYSTATION)

Appreciation for the level design skyrocketed as you realised that the whole quest was about to play out again, now with the floors on the ceilings.

68
SUPER MARIO WORLD 2: YOSHI'S ISLAND
(1995, NINTENDO, SNES)

Baby Bowser: pushover. Then Kamek turned him into a fire-spitting monstrosity lumbering closer by the second. Egg his face! EGG HIS FACE!

67
COUNTER-STRIKE
(2000, SIERRA, PC)

Now here's a bomb defusal map with legs! Ready for the mad dash to lock down that hallway chokepoint? You'd better be...

66
PORTAL 2
(2011, VALVE, PC)

"Oh. It's you." Quirky and murderous as ever, nothing felt cheap about reactivating Portal's QA supercomputer gone off the rails.

65
GEARS OF WAR
(2006, MICROSOFT, 360)

This 18-rated game deserved its classification. If you're old enough, it's a fantastic but grisly experience. If not, stay away!

64
FAR CRY
(2004, UBISOFT, PC)

Let loose on a tropical island, empowered by Crytek's CryEngine, you could go anywhere and come at your objectives from any angle. A new class of sandbox gaming had arrived.

63
FINAL FANTASY VI
(1994, SQUARE, SNES)

Celes took part in a fully-fledged tragic opera - with a few prompts from you and assistance from the rest of the party in fending off a finale-crashing purple octopus, live on stage.

62
THE HITCHHIKER'S GUIDE TO THE GALAXY
(1984, INFOCOM, PC)

Successfully acquiring this thing took a setup elaborate enough to make a Bond baddie weep with envy. Text adventures! They don't make 'em like that any more.

61
THE LEGEND OF ZELDA: WIND WAKER
(2002, NINTENDO, GAMECUBE)

After an intense game of parry, strike and dodge, the killing blow was made right between Ganondorf's evil eyes in this beautiful outing for Link.

60
BATMAN: ARKHAM CITY
(2011, Warner Bros, 360)

He's dead! He's alive! No, he's dead. And thanks to the Titan formula, Bats didn't even need to get his hands dirty.

59
BRAID
(2008, MICROSOFT, 360)

Going for the final secret star meant blowing up the princess in the process. Oopsie.

THE LEGEND OF ZELDA: WIND WAKER

CASTLEVANIA: SYMPHONY OF THE NIGHT

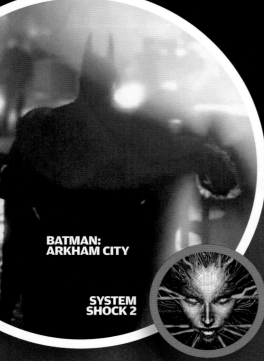

BATMAN:
ARKHAM CITY

SYSTEM
SHOCK 2

52
WORMS 2: ARMAGEDDON
(1999, MICROPROSE, PC)
Most gangsta way to kill an enemy Worm: prod them off a cliff into the sea. Just don't let it happen to you.

51
DOOM
(1993, ID, PC)
Going toe-to-hoof with the Cyberdemon. Although outranked by Hell's Spiderdemon, the rocket-toting Cyberdemon encountered on Mars's moon Deimos still felt like Doom's true boss.

50
UNCHARTED 3: DRAKE'S DECEPTION
(2011, SONY, PS3)
Serious mid-air James Bond heroics and a million-to-one escape removed any thoughts that this series was running out of ideas.

49
MAX PAYNE
(2001, 3D REALMS, PC)
Two years after The Matrix blew us away at the cinema, Remedy squeezed the magic of slow-mo bullet time into Max's shooter. It not only made for the best gunfights we'd ever seen, it changed the face of gaming forever as dozens copied it.

48
STARWING
(1993, NINTENDO, SNES)
Brilliant scientist turned telekinetic screwball, Andross's floating space face was a huge shocker in the SNES days.

47
PHOENIX WRIGHT: ACE ATTORNEY: TRIALS AND TRIBULATIONS
(2007, NINTENDO, NINTENDO DS)
After dozens of hours of carefully-woven character development, the third Phoenix Wright game drew all the plot devices together by having the most popular antagonists team up to take down the baddie when Feenie's in hospital. A breathtaking example of giving the fans exactly what they want.

46
THE ELDER SCROLLS IV: OBLIVION
(2006, 2K GAMES, PC)
Stepping out from the dank, linear sewer system into the bright world of Cyrodiil was a moment that defined Oblivion.

45
WORLD OF WARCRAFT
(2004, BLIZZARD, PC)
Although the game's packed with hundreds of personal moments, the C'Thun raid's staggering difficulty (now blunted with patches, somewhat) made it an iconic battle.

44
THE LEGEND OF ZELDA: A LINK TO THE PAST
(1991, NINTENDO, SNES)
Everything you thought you knew about Zelda was wrong when Link warped into the Dark World and entered an all-new Hyrule. We still get goosebumps when we think about how the game's size doubled in that instant.

43
SUPER STREET FIGHTER II TURBO
(1994, CAPCOM, ARCADE)
Even seeing the first and most fearsome hidden character in Street Fighter history was a challenge. Being able to beat him was a whole other matter...

42
REZ
(2001, SEGA, DREAMCAST)
The end of Rez's fourth level is crazy like no other: a loopy battle against a swirl of nodes that transform into a running man. A creative triumph.

41
CHRONO CROSS
(1999, SQUARE, PLAYSTATION)
The deception was perfect: what threat could a country bumpkin ever pose to a squad of weathered fighters? More of a threat than any other, it turned out, in a chilling battle in front of a clanging bell.

40
RESIDENT EVIL
(1996, CAPCOM, PLAYSTATION)
Anybody who claims they didn't jump when the Cerberus zombie-dog burst through the windows is a fibber. Capcom slyly remixed the scene for the GameCube's REmake, too. Absolutely terrifying in a way that many in the series to replicate, as well as plenty of other games like Silent Hill.

58
MEDAL OF HONOR: ALLIED ASSAULT
(2002, EA, PC)
If there was ever a combat situation not to be in... but knowing what was ahead made you more determined to somehow scramble through it alive.

57
GTA: VICE CITY
(2002, ROCKSTAR, PS2)
True, the game may not have caught on if they'd called it Noise Pollution: Vice City. But that didn't take anything away from the amazing music as you cruised the sunny streets, speakers pumping out V-Rock or Fever 105.

56
LEFT 4 DEAD
(2008, VALVE, PC)
Never what you'd call lighthearted knockabout fun, the limited visibility, zombie hordes and potential for ambush, gunfire and panic here ran roughshod over the nerves.

55
SYSTEM SHOCK 2
(1999, EA, PC)
Pulling the wool with that old who's-the-bad-guy trick. Full credit to developers Irrational, it was still pretty damn slick when they pulled the same trick in BioShock.

54
EARTHBOUND
(1994, NINTENDO, SNES)
Now here's a boss battle. You couldn't kill this terrifying alien freakshow, so what did you do? Inspired half the cast of the game to pray him out of existence, that's what. Gobsmacking.

53
BATTLEFIELD 1942
(2002, EA, PC)
Classic horseshoe Pacific map and Battlefield series icon. First or 500th time, you're guaranteed it won't be a dull skirmish.

STARWING

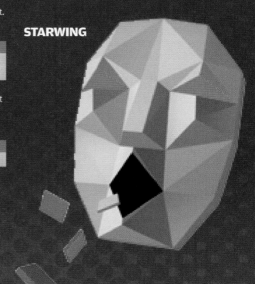

SUPER MARIO WORLD

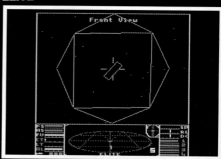

ELITE

33
STAR WARS: KNIGHTS OF THE OLD REPUBLIC
(2003, LUCASARTS, XBOX)

Traditionally Star Wars has always been a good versus bad story, but KOTOR flipped expectations by casting you as The Dark Lord of the Sith: albeit a brainwashed one. The revelation was masterfully handled, and the freedom to return to the Dark Side was nothing short of genius.

32
SSX 3
(2003, EA, PS2)

Unlocking the final peak in SSX 3 gave us something even current-gen SSX can't offer: one long interrupted snowboarding session from the summit of the mountain down to the base. It's a gargantuan ride like being strapped to an adrenaline pump.

31
HALF-LIFE
(1998, SIERRA, PC)

Half-Life hero Gordon Freeman isn't a space marine or a kung fu master. He's a regular scientist who got caught up in an inter-dimensional blowout while going about his regular-ish science job. Half-Life's low-key opening wisely lets you appreciate this as you quietly ride to work.

30
PONG
(1972, ATARI, ARCADE)

For many, Pong was the entry point to a lifetime of gaming. Actually controlling an on-screen paddle was nothing short of a revelation, and using it to score your first point is a memory no gamer should be without.

29
METROID
(1986, NINTENDO, NES)

Back in '86 the truth about Samus's gender was a slap in the face of everyone closed-minded enough to think female game characters were only for rescuing.

28
ELITE
(1984, ACORNSOFT, BBC MICRO)

Manually docking a spaceship: a borderline-painful test of skill that demanded pinpoint precision. The tough moments are always the most rewarding.

METROID

39
MISSILE COMMAND
(1980, ATARI, ARCADE)

Atari put the weight of the entire world on your shoulders in Cold War coin-op Missile Command. Fail to meet the challenge and the planet blew up in a fizz of noise and colour.

38
ICO
(2001, SONY, PS2)

The silent relationship between Ico and Yorda was as pure as they come, and when the pair were separated by a parting bridge there was nothing to be done. Or was there? Without a moment's hesitation we all found ourselves leaping over to a stranded Yorda and putting our lives in her hands for once.

37
HALO 3
(2007, MICROSOFT, 360)

You face multiple walking tanks throughout Halo 3, and each fight is unique. Like any good boss there are obvious weak points, but the brilliance of the scarab fights is the freedom to pick and choose between them.

36
SUPER MARIO WORLD
(1990, NINTENDO, SNES)

For all his power-ups and suits, Mario's core mechanics never changed. Then Yoshi happened and everything changed. Suddenly the plumber became a mounted god, and the baddies of Dinosaur Land didn't stand a chance.

35
THIEF: DEADLY SHADOWS
(2004, EIDOS, PC)

Regarded by many as the single greatest level of the last ten years, the abandoned Cradle orphanage-turned-insane-asylum is a curveball creation filled with spooks and crazy contraptions.

34
CONKER'S BAD FUR DAY
(2001, RARE, N64)

Battling the Great Mighty Poo?! Launching toilet rolls into the mouth of a giant operatic bum torpedo?!

27
PRINCE OF PERSIA: SANDS OF TIME
(2003, UBISOFT, PS2)

Sands of Time's rewind idea let Ubisoft create unthinkable traps, and being able to magically undo your errors gave you the confidence to tackle them.

26
THE DARKNESS
(2007, 2K GAMES, 360)

Proving it's not all guns and gore, Starbreeze let us sit on the sofa and watch the entirety of To Kill a Mockingbird on the tiny TV set if we so chose. And we did.

25
FALLOUT 3
(2008, BETHESDA, PC)

You find the city of Megaton early on: it's a ramshackle town built around an unexploded nuclear bomb. Accept an attractive contract from a Mr Tenpenny and you'll find yourself reactivating the bomb and detonating it from afar, completely wiping one of the Capital Wastelands's main locations!

24
POKÉMON RED/BLUE
(1996, NINTENDO, GAME BOY)

Choosing your starting Pokémon and catching your first critter are both huge moments, but the path towards becoming a Pokémon master only really begins when you beat gym leader Brock and get the first of eight badges.

23
SONIC THE HEDGEHOG 2
(1992, SEGA, MEGA DRIVE)

Sonic's transformation into the golden Super Sonic was perfect reward for hours spent hunting down all seven Chaos Emeralds. That first taste of invincibility turned the formerly hostile Westside Island into a giant playground free.

22
RED DEAD REDEMPTION
(2010, ROCKSTAR, 360)

After a long riverboat shootout, John Marston steps over the border and climbs onto his horse for a long ride across Mexico. As the sun sets in the distance and paints the sky a gorgeous golden orange, Jose Gonzalez's song 'Far Away' majestically kicks in from out of nowhere. Masterful.

21
MORTAL KOMBAT
(1992, MIDWAY, ARCADE)

Mortal Kombat will forever be remembered as THE game with THOSE kills. Nasty, but if you're old enough, an iconic moment in gaming history.

HALO:
COMBAT
EVOLVED

BIOSHOCK

20
BIOSHOCK
(2007, 2K GAMES, 360)

Games have the power to transport you into worlds like no other. In the case of Bioshock, that happened with a bathysphere ride down to the ocean depths and into the tragic underwater city known as Rapture.

19
HALO: COMBAT EVOLVED
(2001, MICROSOFT, XBOX)

Halo almost single-handedly rewrote the first-person shooter rulebook, and it was fourth level The Silent Cartographer that had a big hand in doing so. Sure the two-weapon system and the grenade button were showcased much earlier in the game, but the freedom to approach the fourth level in a manner you saw fit - and to completely ignore orders if you fancied a drive - remains the best moment from any Halo game.

18
BATMAN: ARKHAM ASYLUM
(2009, EIDOS, 360)W

In the first two Scarecrow encounters, deadly toxin warps Batman's mind and makes him see things that aren't real. Third time round it's your mind that's being warped as your console appears to suffer a critical graphics-chip overload before the game resets back to the opening movie. It's only when you realise that the roles of Batman and Joker have been switched that you understand it's all a dirty trick.

17
FINAL FANTASY VII
(1997, SQUARE, PLAYSTATION)

When the most iconic Final Fantasy bad guy in history meets the pretty flower girl who has faithfully stood by your side there was only ever going to be one outcome. Even so, her death still chokes us up.

16
THE SECRET OF MONKEY ISLAND
(1990, LUCASARTS, PC)

With more jokes per square second (whatever the heck one of those is) than any other game, the old point'n'click classic is brimming with laughs. Some stand out more than others, though, and they all stem from verbal duelling as Guybrush wraps his tongue around the lost art of insult sword fighting.

15
METAL GEAR SOLID 3: SNAKE EATER
(2004, KONAMI, PS2)

Taking down sniping superstar The End took the best part of an hour if you failed to get him earlier in the game. But there was another way: the old codger was so close to death's door anyway that fast-forwarding the PS2's internal clock by a week resulted in the wiry opponent croaking it from old age.

14
TETRIS
(1989, NINTENDO, GAME BOY)

You waited ages for a long stack of four blocks to arrive and then two came along at once. But if you were playing it smart, you'd have left a thin chimney to drop them in. Obliterating four rows in an instant is fist-pump-worthy stuff; doubly so if you could combo it.

13
GRAND THEFT AUTO 3
(2001, ROCKSTAR, PS2)

It would be easy to create a list of 250 great moments from the Grand Theft Auto series as a whole, and there's even a good case for plucking just as many stand out bits from GTA 3 alone it's so chock full of memorable events. And at the very top of that list would be working your way up the wanted rating by piling up the bad deeds until you hit the full six stars. It was clearly a futile and pointless act, as very few could survive that final stand against the army, but of course it was the taking part that counted.

12
COD 4: MODERN WARFARE
(2007, ACTIVISION, 360)

Modern Warfare's signature level was all smoke and mirrors. The level was nothing but you following very precise orders from your guide. The set-pieces were the most scripted set-pieces imaginable. And yet the infiltration of Pripyat - from the tank field to the dog stare-off - guaranteed sweaty palms. Often imitated, never equalled.

11
METAL GEAR SOLID
(1998, KONAMI, PLAYSTATION)

There's no other boss like him. The Psycho Mantis fight was the ultimate in convention-smashing gameplay as the resident FOXHOUND psychic telegraphed your moves and commented on your past gaming preferences by sneaking a peek at your memory card's save data. Cleverly, yanking out the controller and plugging it into the second port tipped the scales in your favour by leaving 'Mantis flailing without a mind to latch onto.

10
DONKEY KONG
(1981, NINTENDO, ARCADE)

The first level of Donkey Kong is one of the most celebrated gaming images in history, and it's not hard to understand why. The ability to hurdle over barrels was so progressive Nintendo only went and called the game's hero Jumpman.

9
HALF-LIFE 2
(2004, VALVE, PC)

Grabbing the gravity gun in Half-Life 2 was an incredible moment for shooters: the point at which physics became a core part of game design. Half-Life 2 was built around this one weapon, and the first chance to really put it through its paces came in the zombified town of Ravenholme. Forget guns: saw blades, gas tanks and traps were all you needed in a level that's as much about puzzle-solving as it is about killing.

8
PAC-MAN
(1980, NAMCO, ARCADE)

The lasting image of Pac-Man is that of a hungry adventurer being chased by ghosts. But swallowing one of the four power pills could flip everything on its head and turn hunted into hunter. The frightened look on the ghosts' faces, their spectral chops now sporting a bluish tint as they frantically glided away, and the awesome sight of their disembodied eyes floating around after digestion are simply unforgettable.

7
GOLDENEYE 007
(1997, NINTENDO, N64)

Beginning with the most famous vent in videogames, the Facility level saw millions of Bonds worldwide shoot millions of hats off of millions of guards perched on millions of toilets. The fun didn't stop there, as poison vats and scientists in Daz-white lab coats played their part in James Bond's best gaming moment to date. By a country mile.

6
PORTAL
(2007, VALVE, PC)

By Portal's finale you'd broken out of the Aperture test chambers and listened to GLaDOS's increasingly-crazy rants. The only thing left to do is to pull her apart: something done personality trait by personality trait. Her character deconstruction manages to tread the fine line between comedy and tragedy without faltering, and once dead, your reward is nothing short of the best credits sequence ever created in the history of things: Jonathan Coulton's Still Alive song.

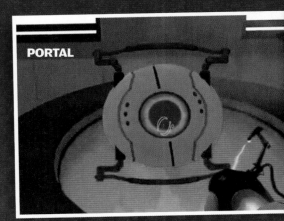

PORTAL

SHADOW OF THE COLOSSUS
(2005, SONY, PS2)

Thirteen: it's unlucky for some, but not us gamers, as the 13th colossus flies high above all others. Phalanx is a soaring sand-serpent and the most docile of all the game's leviathans. Even getting onto its back takes a cunning mind and exceptional skill. Taking it down is a whole other problem...

4

SONIC & KNUCKLES
(1994, SEGA, MEGA DRIVE)

Sonic & Knuckles was a brilliant game on its own, but the adventure on its cartridge was just the beginning (well, technically the end) of its fun. Flipping open the top hatch and slotting the older Sonics down onto the circuitry created all-new takes on the earlier games – with Sonic 3 in particular designed with the lock-on features in mind. In one clunking motion SEGA breathed new life into old games, and revisiting Sonic 2 and 3 with Knuckles led to hours upon hours of brand new content and secrets.

3

THE LEGEND OF ZELDA: OCARINA OF TIME
(1998, NINTENDO, N64)

Hyrule field: it's had many incarnations over the decades, but its most famous of all came in Ocarina of Time. It was a gargantuan space to cross on foot, but adult Link had a trick up his sleeve. After befriending Epona as a child he was able to break her out of her prison and release her into the wild. So began the most iconic Zelda friendship of all, and a chance to ride across Hyrule's plains in tandem with the stirring day/night cycle.

2

RESIDENT EVIL 4
(2005, CAPCOM, GAMECUBE)

It's for over 18's only, but Resident Evil 4's early village attack is the birthplace of the modern action game. It's where clunky cameras and awkward aiming mechanics were given the heave-ho in favour of polished feature sets. It's where the over-the-shoulder cam came into prominence, and the ability to individually target bits of enemies really became useful. It's also the reason why we have multiple action button prompts pop up in all manner of games.

But more than that, it was where we met the sack-head Dr Salvador and had our heads chopped off in the blink of an eye. And where, no matter where we ran, how many ladders we kicked down, or what blockades we constructed, the enemies just didn't stop coming. It was where horrible housewives flanked us from around the houses. It was where fear was reborn, and where action games reached their pinnacle. It was where gaming enjoyed its finest ever moment, apart from one other...

SUPER MARIO 64

(1996, NINTENDO, N64)

If you've played games, you've started wars, won world cup finals, conquered worlds. So how did merely running around for a bit at the start of a game become the Greatest Gaming Moment? Well you had to be there in 1996 to experience the sheer delight of seeing Mario's world made real in three dimensions for the first time. As someone wrote back then, until that point it was like you'd only received flat postcards from this place and now you were actually there. It was beautifully set up too. There's the most fun intro screen ever with a startling 3D Mario head to pull around like a naughty toddler and then a swooping fly-by of the castle and an introduction to camera man Laikatu, all designed to reassure you about the unfamiliar analogue controls and new, eye-opening perspective. And then with a push of the stick you send Mario tiptoeing, then walking, then running with outstretched arms into the next dimension of gaming. Triple jumping for joy with a "Wahoo!", has the average player's emotions ever matched the character on screen's quite so perfectly? And all that's before you entered the castle and wondered what would happen if you jumped into those paintings...

PROFILE

iHasCupquake

Real Name: Tiffany Herrera
Channel: youtube.com/c/ihascupquakeplus
Famous for... Her animated videos, and DIY and baking skills.

INSTAGRAM

A shoot for Cosmic Confetti. We think she looks like Lady Gaga here!

Paying a visit to Toy Box Collectibles. We want all of these! Like, now!

Entering an Alice Through The Looking Glass contest to tie in with the film!

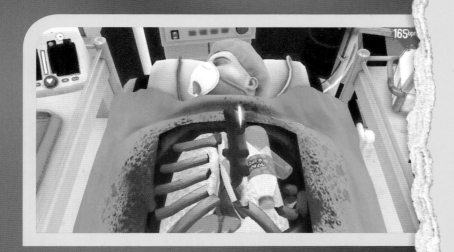

FAVOURITE GAME

Surgeon Simulator

It's surprisingly difficult to control your own hands, so what can possibly go wrong when you need to do a double kidney transplant in a corridor?

VITAL STATS

Channel start date:
19 August 2010
Subscriber count:
4,631,269
Most watched video:
Five Nights At Freddy's animated short

HEY GUYS!

1 **Careless Chub Moves**
Cupquake and her husband have a dance off while wearing amazing inflatable suits.

2 **DIY TNT Block Candle**
This is a really effective and easy crafty project that we can't wait to try ourselves. It involves a cutting board and glue gun, so you may need adult help!

OUR FAVE

3 **Notice Me Senpai**
The animation in this vid is super cute, and yet somehow scary with how quickly it turns nasty!

100 GAMES SHOOK

Join us as we run down our epic collection of the most

Videogames have come a long way over the years, and there have been many lists written about games. This is different though. This is not a list of the best games, nor of the games you should crack out and give a go right now (though you'd earn yourself a gaming education by doing so). No. These the most important, most *influential* games of all time. The games that changed the course of gaming. That shook the world, no less!

100
E.T. THE EXTRA-TERRESTRIAL
Format Atari 2600
Pub Atari **Dev** Atari
Year 1982

You can't deny its cultural significance – a game so bad it crashed the '80s video game industry and had to be buried in bulk in the desert.

99
DEMON'S SOULS
Format PS3
Pub Namco Bandai
Dev From Software
Year 2009

Effectively a Dark Souls prototype that established the series' unique tone and approach – and Miyazaki's place in the industry.

98
CHRONO TRIGGER
Format SNES **Pub** Square
Dev Square **Year** 1995

An epic JRPG that changed the genre with its branching story and replayability.

97
GEOMETRY WARS
Format 360, Xbox **Pub** Microsoft
Dev Bizarre Creations **Year** 2003

Originally a minigame in Project Gotham Racing, this twin-stick shooter was responsible for popularising XBLA and digital downloads on consoles.

96
ASSASSIN'S CREED II
Format PC, PS3, 360, Xbox **Pub** Ubisoft
Dev Ubisoft
Year 2007

Introduced the charismatic Ezio Auditore and refined the sandbox template for a generation and beyond via Venice, Florence, and Tuscany.

95
BALDUR'S GATE II
Format PC **Pub** Black Isle
Dev Bioware **Year** 2000

You led a party of six in this early, pre-Mass Effect/Dragon Age showcase of Bioware's skill at creating unforgettable characters and densely layered narratives.

94
MEGA MAN
Format NES **Pub** Capcom
Dev Capcom **Year** 1987

While most players got to grips with gaming via plumbers and hedgehogs, Mega Man gave many their first real challenge. Notable also for being one of the first focal points for speed-runners.

93
EARTHBOUND
Format SNES **Pub** Nintendo
Dev Ape, HAL Laboratories **Year** 1994

A cult classic, which cemented Nintendo great Satoru Iwata as a programming legend and proved one of the formative JRPGs of the NES era.

92
GUITAR HERO
Format PS2 **Pub** Red Octane
Dev Harmonix **Year** 2005

The title that made big plastic peripherals profitable, popularised rhythm action, and gave music a proper videogame platform.

91
METROID PRIME
Format GameCube **Pub** Nintendo
Dev Retro Studios **Year** 2002

One of the most successful genre conversions ever, letting you step more immersively into Samus' space shoes than ever before.

THAT THE WORLD

influential, most important games ever...

90
UNREAL TOURNAMENT
Format PC
Pub GT Interactive
Dev Epic **Year** 1999

Seriously fast, furious, and satisfying first-person shooting that set a new benchmark for competitive PvP action in videogames.

89
RED DEAD REDEMPTION
Format PS3, 360
Pub Rockstar Games
Dev Rockstar San Diego
Year 2010

So much more than just GTA in the Wild West, Red Dead's world felt uniquely authentic and alive. To this day fans still cry out for a sequel.

88
ULTIMA
Format Apple II
Pub Origin Systems
Dev Richard Gariott
Year 1981

One of the first commercially available RPGs, Richard Garriott's adventure fused first-person dungeon-crawling with a top-down open world in a way never before seen.

87
TONY HAWK'S PRO SKATER
Format PS1
Pub Activision
Dev Neversoft **Year** 1999

Addictive score-attack skating responsible for turning an underground counterculture into a bona-fide mainstream craze.

86
THE ELDER SCROLLS IV: OBLIVION
Format PC, PS3, 360 **Pub** Bethesda
Dev Bethesda **Year** 2006

Here Bethesda truly set the template for its open-worlds, with a title that combined spectacle and freedom to an unprecedented degree.

85
SYSTEM SHOCK 2
Format PC **Pub** EA
Dev Irrational Games **Year** 1999

This early step in Bioshock developer Ken Levine's career combined the FPS and RPG genres like never before.

84
KING'S QUEST
Format IBM PCjr **Pub** IBM
Dev Sierra On-Line **Year** 1983

Kick-started the golden era of adventure games, with clever puzzles, pioneering pseudo-3D environments, and trailblazing animation.

83
MYST
Format Mac **Pub** Broderbund
Dev Cyan **Year** 1993

This point-and-clicker put players on a mysterious, puzzle-filled island. Its stunning backgrounds were a massive achievement at the time, and helped introduce a whole new audience to the world of gaming.

82
STAR WARS KOTOR
Format Xbox **Pub** LucasArts
Dev Bioware **Year** 2003

Modern Bioware starts with this incredible RPG, which ultimately inspired the studio to create its own sci-fi universe.

81
THE LEGEND OF ZELDA: LINK'S AWAKENING
Format Game Boy **Pub** Nintendo
Dev Nintendo **Year** 1993

One of Nintendo's prized creators, Yoshiaki Koizumi (creator of Super Mario Galaxy) cut his teeth on this fantastic portable take on Zelda.

80
MAX PAYNE
Format PC, Xbox, PS2 **Pub** Rockstar
Dev Remedy **Year** 2001

Popularised bullet-time battles with its balletic, John Woo-inspired combat.

79
DEVIL MAY CRY
Format PS2 **Pub** Capcom
Dev Capcom **Year** 2001

Fluid hack-and-slashing that invented the genre the likes of Bayonetta and Metal Gear Rising Revengeance would later occupy.

78
METAL GEAR SOLID 3: SNAKE EATER
Format PS2 **Pub** Konami
Dev Konami **Year** 2004

Big Boss donned camouflage and answered the call of nature for Kojima's stealthy prequel, with inspirational new survival mechanics.

77
COMMAND & CONQUER
Format PC **Pub** EA
Dev Westwood Studios
Year 1995

Several playable factions in parallel campaigns gave real-time strategy a kick up the bum.

76
BRAID
Format 360
Pub Microsoft
Dev Number None
Year 2008

Space-time-altering puzzles and a multi-faceted story widened the horizons of indie development, and this remains a landmark 'art game'.

75
POPULOUS
Format PC, SNES, Mega Drive, Game Boy, Master System, Amiga, Atari ST
Pub EA **Dev** Bullfrog Productions **Year** 1989

A single title that established not only the god game as a genre, but the status of Peter Molyneux as a game designer.

74
UNCHARTED 2
Format PS3 **Pub** Sony
Dev Naughty Dog **Year** 2009

Swashbuckling set pieces, globetrotting drama, and sheer visual spectacle in one polished package that changed triple-A games forever.

73
THEME PARK
Format PC, PS1, Saturn, Jaguar, 3DO, Mega CD, SNES, Mega Drive, Amiga **Pub** EA
Dev Bullfrog Productions **Year** 1994

Bullfrog's management sim substituted spreadsheet complexity for streamlined quirkiness, paving the way for the raft of jaunty administration games to come, now so common from the App Store to Early Access.

72
SUPER SMASH BROS
Format N64 **Pub** Nintendo
Dev HAL Laboratory **Year** 1999

Smash Bros. came out of leftfield to invent the mascot brawler, popularise the four-player fighting game, and open up the genre to Joe Public.

71
EVERQUEST
Format PC **Pub** Sony
Dev Sony **Year** 1999

It may not have been the first fantasy MMO, but Everquest's popularity cast a mould for the genre.

70
FIFA 09
Format PC, Mobile, PS3, Wii, 360, PSP, DS, Xbox, PS2
Pub EA **Dev** EA Canada **Year** 2008

The birth of Ultimate Team changed sports games forever, and is a staple to this day.

69
LEMMINGS
Format PC, Amiga CD32, SNES, CD-I, Game Gear, Mega Drive, Game Boy, Master System, NES, Amiga, Atari ST, Amstrad CPC, C64, Spectrum
Pub Psygnosis **Dev** DMA Design **Year** 1991

A triumph of open-ended design from the studio that would go on to make Grand Theft Auto.

68
THIEF: THE DARK PROJECT
Format PC **Pub** Eidos Interactive
Dev Looking Glass Studios **Year** 1998

Throwing out confrontation for light and sound-based stealth, this steampunk sneaker also introduced gamers to Ken Levine's writing.

67
RATCHET & CLANK
Format PS2 **Pub** Sony
Dev Insomniac Games **Year** 2002

A colourful fusion of platforming and action, and a graphical showcase for Sony's hardware.

66
JAK & DAXTER: THE PRECURSOR LEGACY
Format PS2 **Pub** Sony
Dev Naughty Dog **Year** 2001

The starting point of Naughty Dog's crazed technical ambition was this seamless, connected world of 3D platforming stages.

65
BANJO-KAZOOIE
Format N64 **Pub** Nintendo
Dev Rare **Year** 1998

Rare's attempts to beat Nintendo at its own 3D platforming game produced this wildly imaginative outing.

64
CRASH BANDICOOT
Format PS1 **Pub** Sony
Dev Naughty Dog **Year** 1996

Sony's answer to Mario and Sonic, and the first indication of Naughty Dog's knack for spectacle.

63
HALF-LIFE
Format PC **Pub** Sierra Entertainment
Dev Valve **Year** 1998

An experiment in world building that revolutionised narrative in games by removing cutscenes in favour of environmental storytelling.

62
BIOSHOCK
Format PC, PS3, 360 **Pub** 2K Games
Dev 2K Boston **Year** 2007

2K's horror opus brought clever philosophising to the triple-A shooter, and proved a demand for intelligent blockbusters in the process.

61
THE LEGEND OF ZELDA: A LINK TO THE PAST
Format SNES Pub Nintendo
Dev Nintendo EAD Year 1992

The game that perfected and cemented the Zelda template, as well as establishing a dual worlds motif that many games would go on to pinch.

60
QUAKE
Format PC, N64, Saturn, Amiga Pub GT Interactive
Dev Id Software Year 1996

Doom may have popularised the FPS, but Quake brought the genre a giant leap closer to its current form, introducing fully 3D environments and accumulating a community of online deathmatch fans.

59
FINAL FANTASY X
Format PS2 Pub Sony
Dev Square Year 2002

Square's PS2 debut ditched the traditional JRPG overworld in favour of lavish 3D environments and a fully voice-acted narrative, establishing a new template for role-playing epics.

58

PRINCE OF PERSIA: SANDS OF TIME
Format PC, GameCube, Xbox, PS2 Pub: Ubisoft
Dev Ubisoft Montreal
Year 2003

The wall-running royal augmented his acrobatics with the ability to rewind time, a power that's been pilfered by all sorts of games ever since.

57
MORTAL KOMBAT
Format PC, Mega CD, SNES, Game Gear, Mega Drive, Game Boy, Master System, Amiga, Arcade Pub Virgin
Dev Midway Games Year 1992

A fighting game so violent at the time that it essentially spawned modern videogame rating systems. 18 only.

56
ELITE
Format PC, NES, Amiga, Atari ST, Amstrad CPC, C64, Spectrum, BBC Micro Pub Acornsoft
Dev Ian Bell, David Braben Year 1984

A pioneering work of open-ended design, inviting players to explore an enormous universe of seemingly endless possibility.

55
RESIDENT EVIL
Format PC, PS1, Saturn Pub Capcom
Dev Capcom Year 1996

Shuffling zombies, scarce resources, tank controls, and fixed camera angles – this was the game that defined a genre for a decade.

54
LEFT 4 DEAD
Format PC, 360 Pub Valve
Dev Turtle Rock Studios Year 2008

Co-op was nothing new in 2008, but this shooter ditched epic narrative in favour of an AI 'director' to ensure every playthrough felt fresh.

53
HALO 2
Format Xbox Pub Microsoft
Dev Bungie Year 2004

Established not just the template for online shooters on console, but also Xbox Live itself.

52
SUPER MARIO KART
Format SNES Pub Nintendo
Dev Nintendo EAD Year 1993

The father of the kart racer – and the series has been fending off all opposition ever since.

51

SUPER MARIO WORLD
Format SNES Pub Nintendo Dev Nintendo EAD Year 1992

Sega may have beat Nintendo to market with the Mega Drive, but Nintendo shot back with perhaps the greatest launch game of any console ever.

50
DIABLO
Format PC, PS1 Pub Ubisoft
Dev Blizzard North Year: 1997

Took a typically sedate genre and gave it a shot of adrenaline, swapping chin-stroking tactics for clickety action and procedural generation.

49
WOLFENSTEIN 3D
Format PC, Jaguar, SNES Pub Apogee Software
Dev Id Software Year 1992

Before Doom, this frenetic blaster essentially invented the modern first-person shooter.

48
SILENT HILL 2
Format PC, Xbox, PS2 Pub Konami
Dev Konami Year 2001

Rather than concentrating on jump scares and ammo conservation, Konami's survival horror sequel delivered its shivers by turning inwards, showing the misshapen enemies as projections of the character's damaged mind.

47
OUTRUN
Format Master System, Arcade Pub Sega
Dev Sega AM2 Year 1986

Although top-down 2D racers had been popular for some time, Yu Suzuki's arcade phenomenon offered a peerless sensation of speed by positioning the player right behind the action.

46
PORTAL
Format PC, PS3, 360 Pub Valve
Dev Valve Year 2007

Valve's comedy puzzler wasn't just an astonishing anthology of headscratchers, it was also a masterpiece of focus and restraint, an early example of the possibilities afforded by digital distribution to produce games of all scales.

45

ANIMAL CROSSING
Format GameCube Pub Nintendo
Dev Nintendo Year 2004

Nintendo's experiment in life management ran at its own gentle pace, and expected players to check in regularly for short, soothing sessions – a pattern of play that's since been exploited, for better or worse, by mobile developers.

44
DEUS EX
Format PC, PS2 Pub Eidos Interactive
Dev Ion Storm Year 2000

Today it seems every game is a mongrel, and first-person titles in particular are often hybrid blends of RPG levelling and open-world influences. It was this cyberpunk shooter that set the precedent for today's creative cross-breeds.

43

DONKEY KONG
Format NES, Arcade Pub Nintendo
Dev Nintendo Year 1981

After a handful of moderate successes in the arcade space, this was the game that cemented Nintendo's commitment to gaming and spawned the company's mascot in one fell swoop.

42

BATMAN: ARKHAM ASYLUM

Format PC, PS3, 360 **Pub** Eidos Interactive
Dev Rocksteady Studios **Year** 2009

Rocksteady's take on the Batman didn't just launch a franchise, it served as a major inspiration for just about every third-person action game released since, with its free-flowing combat being nabbed wholesale by any number of other developers.

41

THE SECRET OF MONKEY ISLAND
Format PC, Amiga, Atari ST **Pub** LucasArts
Dev LucasArts **Year** 1990

As well as being a tremendous example of LucasArts' comedy and craft in its own right, Ron Gilbert's piratical adventure shored up the genre foundations that led us all the way to Telltale's The Walking Dead today.

40

WII SPORTS
Format Wii **Pub** Nintendo
Dev Nintendo **Year** 2006

The perfect showcase for the Wii's motion controls, and an app so killer it single-handedly made the console a crossover hit.

39

WIPEOUT
Format PS1 **Pub** Psygnosis
Dev Psygnosis **Year** 1995

With a look brainstormed by graphic designers and a techno soundtrack starring The Chemical Brothers, this future-set anti-gravity racer was PlayStation's style icon.

38

SONIC THE HEDGEHOG
Format Mega Drive **Publisher** SEGA
Dev Sonic Team **Year** 1991

For a time this speedy blue hedgehog was bigger than Mario, and that's down to a platformer-cum-racer that made the competition look positively pedestrian by comparison.

37

MASS EFFECT 2
Format PC, 360, PS3 **Pub** Bioware
Dev Bioware **Year** 2007

The game that defined the Bioware RPG, mixing an expansive, wonderfully-realised universe, engaging dialogues, and a hefty dollop of genuinely affecting moral choices with hard-hitting third-person shooter action.

36

SHENMUE
Format Dreamcast **Pub** SEGA
Dev SEGA AM2 **Year** 1999

Open worlds are ten a penny these days, but back then the chance to wander a fully realised Japanese town, interacting with arcade machines, driving a forklift, and challenging locals to arm wrestling contests, was truly revolutionary.

35

TEAM FORTRESS 2
Format PC, 360, PS3 **Pub** Valve
Dev Valve **Year** 2007

Multiplayer competition that continues to evolve with the times, morphing from a simple class-based shooter to an enormously successful, free-to-play juggernaut, complete with player mods and its own hat-based economy.

34

STARCRAFT
Format PC **Pub** Blizzard
Dev Blizzard **Year** 1998

The real-time strategy game so perfectly competitive that it essentially defined esports forever, and remains South Korea's national obsession to this day.

33

THE LEGEND OF ZELDA
Format NES **Pub** Nintendo
Dev Nintendo **Year** 1986

This fantasy adventure not only helped cement Nintendo as the gaming giant it is today, but laid the groundwork for countless genres to come, from open-world games to RPGs.

32

SHADOW OF THE COLOSSUS
Format PS2 **Pub** Sony
Dev Team Ico **Year** 2005

No game yet has matched this classic's incredible sense of scale, let alone its uniquely melancholy atmosphere and beautifully stark art style – though not for lack of trying.

31

SIMCITY
Format PC, SNES, Amiga, Atari ST **Pub** Maxis
Dev Maxis **Year** 1989

A now sprawling family of Sim games started here, with a city builder that defined the management genre, and popularised open-ended gaming like never before.

30

ANGRY BIRDS
Format Mobile **Pub** Chillingo
Dev Rovio **Year** 2009

Breakout hits don't come much bigger than this casual mobile game turned household name, now so popular there's even a movie on the way.

29

PAC-MAN
Format Arcade **Pub** Namco
Dev Namco **Year** 1980

A triumph of arcade gaming purity that spawned the first true gaming mascot, and made its influence felt on countless genre-defining titles to follow. It's impossible to imagine videogames without it.

28

LEAGUE OF LEGENDS
Format PC **Dev** Riot
Pub Riot **Year** 2009

The latest League Of Legends championship drew millions of fans, and awarded millions more in money to the overall victor. This early MOBA not only popularised what is now one of the most successful genres in gaming, but also helped turn esports into an ever-growing global sensation.

27

CASTLEVANIA: SYMPHONY OF THE NIGHT
Format PS1 **Dev** Konami
Pub Konami **Year** 1997

A darkly gothic platformer which, like Metroid, perfectly melded open-world and linear gameplay with its ability-gated environments. So good they (half) named a genre after it – the Metroidvania.

26
CIVILIZATION
Format PC, Saturn, SNES, Amiga, Atari ST
Dev MPS Labs
Pub MicroProse **Year** 1991

Thousands, if not millions of lives were in your hands as you built your nation from a humble settlement into a network of thriving cities - and witnessed the birth of the modern 4X genre.

25
GRAN TURISMO

Format PS1 **Pub** Sony
Dev Sony **Year** 1997

An authentic car sim in a period when the arcade racer reigned supreme, and the first to make truly realistic racing a mainstream hit. Still an extraordinary title.

24
THE SIMS
Format PC **Pub** EA
Dev Maxis **Year** 2000

Truly progressive, both in its gameplay and its politics, with an inclusive approach that welcomed female gamers and normalised gay marriage. The Sims proved games could be for everyone.

23
GOLDENEYE 007

Format N64 **Pub** Nintendo
Dev Rare **Year** 1997

Rare's gold-standard Bond game brought the previously PC-only first-person shooter, and the definitive splitscreen experience, to consoles. If you owned an N64, chances are you've played deathmatch on Facility.

22
CALL OF DUTY 4: MODERN WARFARE
Format PC, PS3, 360 **Pub** Activision
Dev Infinity Ward **Year** 2007

From its set-piece-driven campaign to a silky 60fps multiplayer that constantly rewarded players with perks and rank-ups, you can thank this classic for shaping almost every multiplayer shooter - and many non-shooters - ever since.

21
MORROWIND
Format PC, Xbox **Pub** Bethesda
Dev Bethesda **Year** 2002

The unrestricted scope and scale of this massive RPG showed gamers exactly what Bethesda was capable of, and its presence can still be felt in the studio's open-world epics today.

20
GEARS OF WAR
Format 360 **Pub** Microsoft
Dev Epic **Year** 2006

From roadie-running, to cover-snapping, to campaign co-op, to brutal multiplayer, this third-person shooter grabbed the genre by the throat and battered it into the shape it still has today - and as an Xbox-exclusive it single-handedly boosted the value of the console.

19
ICO
Format PS2 **Pub** Sony
Dev Team Ico **Year** 2001

Unique, minimalist, and unabashedly elegant, this puzzle-platforming tale of boy meets girl, boy saves girl from castle containing shadow monsters, ruthlessly stripped out anything that detracted from its core conceit, and inspired a generation of developers to see games as art like never before.

18
FINAL FANTASY VII

Format PS1 **Pub** Square
Dev Square **Year** 1997

The JRPG that made western audiences sit up and take notice, and introduced expansive, pre-rendered 3D environments to a previously top-down genre. Aeris' death remains a shared emotional touchstone for gamers everywhere to this day.

17
TOMB RAIDER

Format PS1, Saturn **Pub** Eidos
Interactive **Dev** Core Design **Year** 1996

She may not exactly have been a nuanced feminist icon, looking back, but when this third-person action adventure brought Lara Croft into the world, her role as gaming's female action hero was genuinely revolutionary. Before long she was a household name; videogames' first real celebrity, her face plastered across the cover of even mainstream magazines, and her place in history forever secured.

16
STREET FIGHTER II

Format Arcade, SNES, Mega Drive, Amiga, Atari ST **Pub** Capcom **Dev** Capcom **Year** 1991

The first word, and for many the last, in on-the-couch multiplayer. Taking the first entry's ball and running with it, this tight brawler defined the genre as we know it today with its roster of colourful characters and intense tactical depth. For a good many years, fighting games were king, and that lasting craze can be traced right back here - and, what do you know, its spiritual successor Street Fighter V revived the genre for the present day, too.

15
SUPER METROID

Format SNES **Pub** Nintendo
Dev Intelligent Systems **Year** 1994

The other half of the duo that defined the Metroidvania, this sci-fi platformer is where it all started. Inventive abilities and rewarding exploration made this a game still evoked by the likes of Rocksteady's Batman games today, and spawned a series so enduring it even survived the transition into 3D first-person shooting.

14
WORLD OF WARCRAFT

Format PC **Pub** Blizzard
Dev Blizzard **Year** 2004

This is the highest-grossing videogame of all time, generating over 10 billion dollars since launch and boasting 5.6 million subscribers - and you can see why. Its incredible world and smart, accessible systems set a standard the competition still struggles to meet today, bringing the MMO into the mainstream with such force that even now developers continue to try to hop on its bandwagon.

13
HALF-LIFE 2
Format PC, PS3, 360, Xbox
Pub Valve **Dev** Valve **Year** 2004

"Shooters, meet physics" - that's what Valve said with Half-Life 2. It gave every body and object physical propeties, meaning you could fling saw blades with a Gravity Gun and, to a less violent end, play on some swings. At a time when other FPS games were inert movie sets, this was a world you could influence.

12
PONG
Format Arcade **Pub** Atari
Dev Atari **Year** 1972

The first sports arcade game needs no introduction. Originally a warm-up project for a new Atari employee, it was among the first to escape musty testing backrooms, and essentially launched the industry single-handed by showing other companies that there was money in this new-fangled gaming thing.

11
METAL GEAR SOLID

Format PS1 **Pub** Konami
Dev Konami **Year** 1998

This classic popularised stealth in games, set new standards for quality in sneaking, launched Kojima's career, revolutionised cinematic storytelling in games, and kicked off one of the industry's most popular, long-running series.

10
POKÉMON RED/BLUE
Format Game Boy **Pub** Nintendo
Dev Game Freak **Year** 1999

How could anyone predict that the humble handheld tale of a ten-year-old catching monsters and training them to battle would become Nintendo's biggest franchise by far, eclipsing Zelda, Metroid, and even Mario? There's something universal in the concept, a rare RPG that appeals to people no matter their age or gender. Everyone has a favourite Pokémon, whether it's a cute and cuddly bug or a scary science experiment that wants to kill you. Game Freak smartly capitalised on the addictive quest to 'Catch 'Em All' by spreading the 151 unique monsters across two carts, which popularised trading over link cable. A movie and merchandise machine fronted by the heart-warming face of an electric yellow hamster, that's more successful now than ever, was the result.

9
RESIDENT EVIL 4
Format GameCube, PS2 **Pub** Capcom
Dev Capcom Production Studio 4 **Year** 2005

Capcom's reinvention of its venerable survival horror franchise had far-reaching implications not only for the genre, but for third-person videogames of all kinds. The over-the-shoulder presentation has since become an industry standard, elegantly ushering in a new age of shooter mechanics, and paving the way for the likes of Marcus Fenix and Nathan Drake. But Capcom offered so much more than just a camera angle, delivering a truly cinematic take on the staid conventions of horror videogames while upping the ante in terms of narrative, AI, and grotesque creature design at the same time.

8
TETRIS
Format Game Boy **Pub** Nintendo
Dev Nintendo **Year** 1989

It might have existed in one form or another slightly earlier than the infamous green-tinged monochrome affair that Nintendo cooked up on the cusp of the '90s, but it wasn't until the big N popped this tetromino-tumbling delight into our gaming palms that the world truly clocked onto the delights involved with lining up falling blocks.

The idea, back when the Game Boy launched, was to have Super Mario Land lead the charge, but while Nintendo knew that younger gamers would climb aboard, it was convinced by legendary gaming entrepreneur Henk Rogers (founder of The Tetris Company) that Tetris would be for everyone.

How right they were. Tetris' legacy is vast, ranging from legitimate raving tunes based on the infectious theme song (you'll have it in your head just having read this entry), all the way through to a pocket-busting 425 million-selling smartphone version. And everyone on the planet has a favourite Tetris block, right?

7
HALO
Format PC, Xbox **Pub** Microsoft
Dev Bungie **Year** 2002

While Goldeneye might be credited with popularising the console first-person shooter, Bungie's Xbox launch title was the first to truly nail it, launching as an astoundingly fully-formed implementation of almost everything we associate with the form to this day. Such was its influence that Halo's feature list reads like an inventory of modern FPS trends: recharging shields, trigger-mapped grenades, the two-weapon limit, and gun-butt melee attacks. Halo pioneered them all, along with precise twin-stick controls and a tremendous roster of pilotable vehicles. And as if all that wasn't enough, Halo can also be credited with driving the success of Microsoft's console ambitions, providing the gaming giant with a flagship franchise that endures to this day. To think it was originally planned as an RTS...

6
GRAND THEFT AUTO III
Formats PC, PS2 **Pub** Rockstar
Dev DMA Design **Year** 2001

DMA Design's first foray into the third dimension was such an assured execution of the concept that Liberty City has served as a model of sandbox design for years, as well as kickstarting an industry-wide trend towards open worlds and player freedom that has infiltrated almost the entirety of triple-A gaming. Today's shooters, RPGs, and even racers are all expected to offer us vast playgrounds to tool around in, and the series' longstanding fascination with systems-led game design is proving equally influential in the current generation of games too. Just try to imagine Metal Gear Solid V in a world without GTA III. Unthinkable.

5
MINECRAFT
Format PC, PS4, XO, Wii U, PS3, 360, Vita, Mobile
Pub Mojang **Dev** Mojang **Year** 2009

There's never been a gaming phenomenon like Minecraft. From bedroom project to global sensation, the blocky builder has truly taken the world by storm, and established itself as the defining game of a whole new generation – not just to play, but even to watch, with so much of YouTube dedicated to it that it's putting cute cats out of business.

Procedural generation, crafting, exploration, survival, tools for allowing players to create their own content – Minecraft has established these concepts in gaming more strongly than ever before. Microsoft didn't shell out $2.5 billion for nothing – it's nabbed a share of the future.

THE LEGEND OF ZELDA: OCARINA OF TIME

Formats N64 **Pub** Nintendo
Dev Nintendo EAD **Year** 1998

At this point it's become something of a cliché to recount tales of childhood astonishment at Hyrule Field's scale or Epona's speed and grace. But these well-worn anecdotes are so oft-repeated because they're utterly true; Ocarina's 64-bit Hyrule was an incredible piece of world building, a characterful environ that players got to know inside-out over the course of an epic adventure. Sure, it invented the Z-trigger lock-on, and introduced a boatload of mechanical innovations, but Ocarina Of Time's true legacy is the formidably high bar it set future generations of 3D action-adventure games.

3

SUPER MARIO 64

Format N64 **Pub** Nintendo
Dev Nintendo **Year** 1997

Younger gamers out there might wonder why tired veterans pine for ground-shaking innovations from Nintendo. Before successful experiments with motion controls and other... less successful dabblings, Nintendo wasn't just making games; it was setting industry standards.

Super Mario 64 bought 3D polygons into the spotlight. It gave us dynamic cameras which followed our avatar around whichever direction we chose to go. It gave us 360 degree analog controls via a stick. It gave us gaming's first foundation block for open worlds. Without Super Mario 64, gaming would look very different today. If you ask us, we need Nintendo's next game-changing innovation sharpish, to avoid a future, where Princess Peach's incredible castle, the delights of the triple jump, and Mario's Ravioli-inspired dreams are nothing but a memory...

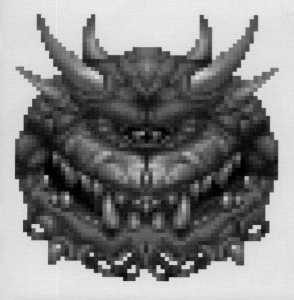

2
DOOM

Formats PC, PS1, Jaguar, SNES **Pub** GT Interactive
Dev Id Software **Year** 1993

Wolfenstein 3D may have laid the groundwork, but Doom was the game that brought the first-person shooter firmly into the mainstream, establishing the genre not only for players, but for money-minded publishers. And while the first-person perspective may be practically ubiquitous in games today, it's easy to forget that there was a time when practically every FPS that came to market was dismissively labelled as a 'Doom clone'. How fortunate, then, that the game that galvanized parsimonious publishers seeking return on investment should have been such an excellent, energetic exercise in supremely satisfying shooting.

1
SUPER MARIO BROS

Format NES **Pub** Nintendo
Dev Nintendo **Year** 1985

In the early 1980s videogames were on the ropes: the market had crashed; revenues had dropped between 1983 and 1985 by a staggering 97% (imagine that portion of today's videogame market suddenly vanishing by 2018). Then along came Ninty, with a plumber-shaped solution.

Super Mario Bros, developed by now legendary designers Shigeru Miyamoto and Takashi Tezuka, was the killer app for the NES. It compelled, through its brilliance, an entire generation of would-be gamers, worn down by rushed tie-ins, to trust in games once more; it delivered on Nintendo's Seal Of Quality, a badge of honour bestowed only to those titles that passed Nintendo's stringent tests; it changed completely people's perspective on the hobby, and birthed a new language for games, featuring design prowess that still holds up some three decades later (see how cack-thumbed most user-created Super Mario Maker levels end up being if you don't believe us). Entire essays have been written about the first few moments, which train you that mushrooms are good and Goombas are bad, and this is a game filled with such slices of incredible design. SMB ensured gaming survived past the '80s, and in the process set the wider industry on a path to greatness. We salute you, Super Mario Bros, for your service to us all – it's our most important game of all time.

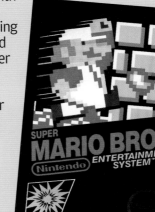

"IT ENSURED GAMING SURVIVED PAST THE '80S, AND SET THE INDUSTRY ON A PATH TO GREATNESS"

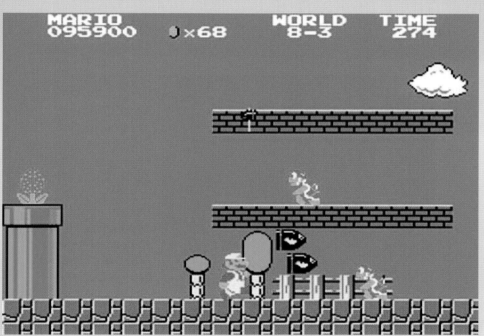

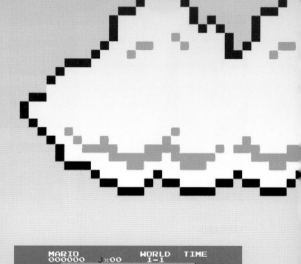

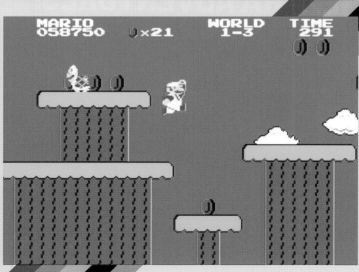

STACYPLAYS VISITS REAL-LIFE
YOUTUBE!

Stacy loves dogs so much that she started a Minecraft series called Dogcraft. In it, she adopts all kinds of virtual puppies, building them dog hotels and even "barkeries" for them to eat at! Yum...

NAME:
STACY HINOJOSA

VLOGGER ID:
STACYPLAYS

SUBSCRIBERS:
1,129,190

CALL FANS:
POTATO FLAKES

MOST VIEWED VIDEO:
WE'RE MERMAIDS! – THE CANY ISLE (EP. 1) 1,999,252 VIEWS

CATCHPHRASE:
GO RESCUE A DOG!

HELLO!

HERE'S Stacy outside YouTube HQ! Check out the shiny sign over on the right. She's off to talk to a room full of people about how she makes her Minecraft videos. What will she be telling them?

EXTRA ADVENTURES!

1 WOW in Stacy's Minecraft series, The Candy Isle, Stacy and her fellow YouTuber AmyLee33 turn into mermaids!

2 SHE'S currently playing Minecraft: Story Mode too! Episode 5's floating sky-city made her gasp out loud.

SHOW AND TELL

SOME bits of Stacy's best videos are shown in the presentation. Everyone laughs at her most hilarious moment, "BIGGEST MINECRAFT HORSE FAIL EVER"! Look it up on YouTube!

FAN-TASTIC

AFTER the event, Stacy meets one of her biggest fans. She's wearing a StacyPlays shirt, and even has a stuffed toy of Molly, Stacy's IRL pet dog and Dogcraft character!

DANCE OFF

TIME for a tour of the YouTube offices. They have fake grass on the roof, basketball hoops indoors, and the meeting rooms are named after viral videos! Remember the Harlem Shake?

CAT SITTER

BUT Stacy loves her animals so much that she can't go a whole day without them... She uses an app to videochat with her cat, Milquetoast, before she goes to sleep. Awwww!

3 FORGET Minecraft diamonds. Stacy recently guest-starred on a YouTube channel called What's Inside? to mine real-life diamond ore.

4 IF YOU love animals, you'll want the new Minecraft mod Stacy helped make. It adds more wolves to your game.

Stampy

Real Name: Joseph Garrett
Channel: youtube.com/user/stampylonghead
Famous for... His cat avatar and ridiculous adventures with his friend Ballistic Squid.

⦿ INSTAGRAM

Playing Xbox in the bath? What on earth are you thinking, Stampy?!

Stampy's cat is always up to mischief - follow on Instagram @stampycatyt!

The cat's real name is Ori, and just loves being in front of the camera!

FAVOURITE GAME

Unravel

Tackle levels and puzzles with a super-cute red woolen creature called Yarny. The story's great and you can't not love the little dude!

VITAL STATS

Channel start date:
29 July 2011
Subscriber count:
7,496,513
Most watched video:
Sinking Feeling

GOODBYYYY YYYYYYYYYYYEEE EEEEEEEE!

BEST VIDS

1 **Flat Challenge**
Stampy builds a super flat world with ridiculous layers (a melon layer?!) and sets himself challenges.

2 **Sinking Feeling**
Stampy starts building a rain-themed ride but soon discovers an unwelcome guest in his world.

OUR FAVE

3 **School Day**
Stampy works his way through various classroom challenges with other YouTube stars as his teachers. Involves lots of cookie eating!

MINECRAFT
MASTERMIND

How much do you really know about your favourite game?

Let's be honest: even your nanna could probably identify a creeper by now. "Is it that scuttly green thing, dear? Ooh, I don't care for him. Best make sure he doesn't go boom." Of course, if you consider yourself to be a Minecraft devotee, your knowledge should probably go a few blocks deeper than that. So take our quiz, and test your trivia smarts...

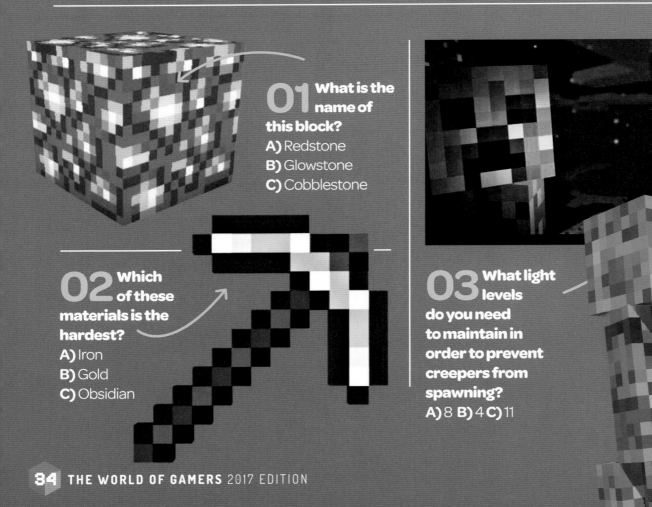

01 What is the name of this block?
A) Redstone
B) Glowstone
C) Cobblestone

02 Which of these materials is the hardest?
A) Iron
B) Gold
C) Obsidian

03 What light levels do you need to maintain in order to prevent creepers from spawning?
A) 8 B) 4 C) 11

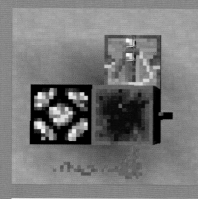

04 How many adjacent blocks can be powered by one block of redstone?

A) 4
B) 2
C) 1

05 How many biomes are there in total?

A) 22
B) 10
C) 16

06 What do you get if you cross a cow and toadstool?

A) Mooshroom
B) Killer bunny
C) Nightmares

07 In what year was the first alpha version of Minecraft released?

A) 2001
B) 2009
C) 2011

08 How many platforms has Minecraft been released on in total?

A) 14
B) 8
C) 12

09 What is the name of the female player character?

A) Joanne
B) Stevena
C) Alex

10 What is the missing ingredient in this cake recipe: sugar, egg, wheat...?
A) Flour
B) Water
C) Milk

11 What is Minecraft creator Notch's real name?
A) Markus Persson
B) Jens Bergensten
C) Daniel Frisk

12 What is the name of the infamous 'ghost' (who does not exist) that some people have claimed to see in Minecraft?
A) Zerowine B) Herobrine C) Spectral Gary

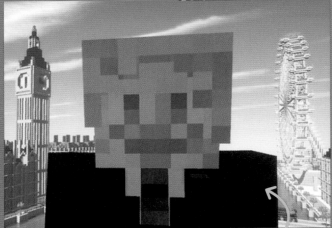

13 Which British politician was recently turned into a Minecraft character?
A) David Cameron
B) Ed Miliband
C) Boris Johnson

16 How many items can you fit in a single chest?
A) 25
B) 27
C) 32

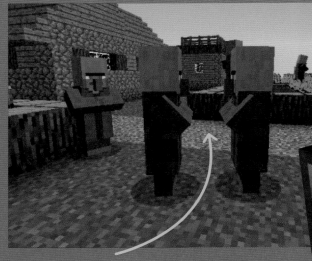

15 What colour eyes do villagers have?
A) Green B) Blue C) Brown

14 Where would you find a zombie pigman?
A) Forest biome
B) The Nether
C) The End

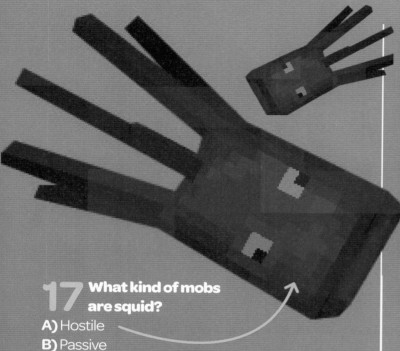

17 What kind of mobs are squid?

A) Hostile
B) Passive
C) Neutral

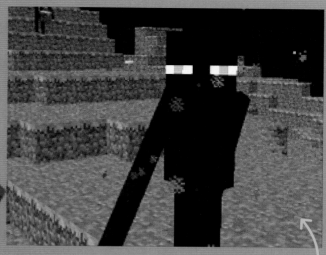

18 Which of these will not stop an enderman from attacking you?

A) Not looking at them
B) Wearing a jack o'lantern
C) Standing still while staring at them

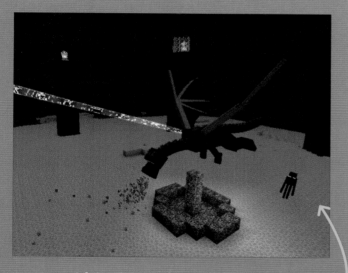

19 Which of these is the most sensible weapon against the Ender Dragon?

A) Bow and arrows **B)** Sword **C)** Axe

20 What was Minecraft's original title?

A) Block Digger **B)** Cave Game
C) Special Steve's Subterranean Adventure

ANSWERS

01: B	09: C	17: B
02: C	10: C	18: C
03: A	11: A	19: A
04: A	12: B	20: B
05: C	13: C	
06: A	14: B	
07: B	15: A	
08: A	16: B	

RESULTS

0-5: Skeleton

Not many Minecraft facts in your mind, are there? Must try harder!

6-10: Villager

You know the lay of the land, but you're not the most adventurous.

11-15: Creeper

You may not be the main man, but you still pack an explosive punch.

16-20: Steve

Top of the blocks. You know the game inside out – well done!

BEST GAMES TO PLAY RIGHT NOW!

Who needs sunshine when you can stay inside and PLAY?!

Brilliant games you should be playing now!

TOWERFALL

Got three friends who are into games? Sweeeet! Multiplayer games are mathematically proven to be properly ace, and there are loads you should try – but none are as cool as Towerfall. It's got arrows, lava, pixel-perfect jumping and a 'just one more go' factor that'll keep you playing until *next* summer!

LEGO THE FORCE AWAKENS

A LEGO tie-in to the best Star Wars film ever is here! You'll get to share the adventure with Finn, Rey and BB-8, see stuff that wasn't in the movie, and – most importantly – hoover up all those lovely studs. Nom! Adventure to page 56 for loads more details!

It's the funniest Lego Star Wars game yet!

SUPER MARIO MAKER

Make your own games with me!

What's better than one Mario game? How about thousands of 'em, created by a community obsessed with the squidgy plumber? And if you get bored of playing, you can spend a month making the hardest level ever!

Wii U

SPLATOON

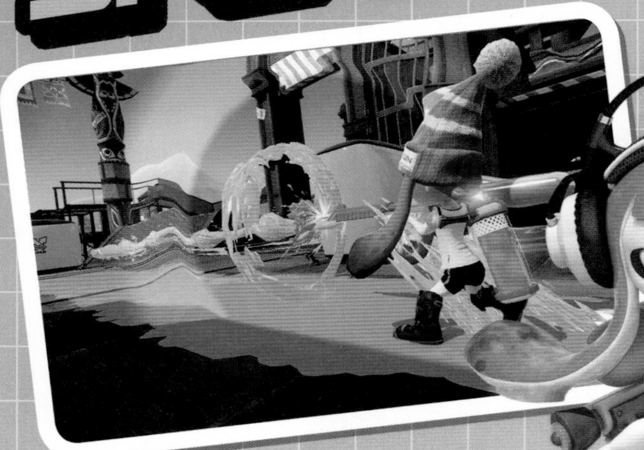

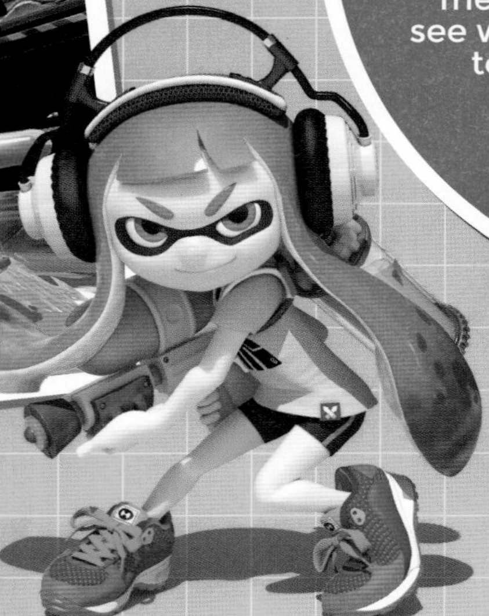

Not all shooting games have to feature blood, bullets and shouty soldiers. Splatoon is gorgeous, bright, gloopy fun, and all those unlockables will keep you busy for months. If only real painting was this enjoyable!

TUBER FAVE

Youtuber DanTDM, who runs The Diamond Minecart channel, recommends Tomodachi Life – a weird, wonderful reality simulator from Nintendo. It plays like a meatier version of their Miitomo mobile app. Create friends, enemies and heroes– then see what happens when they move in together. You've been warned!

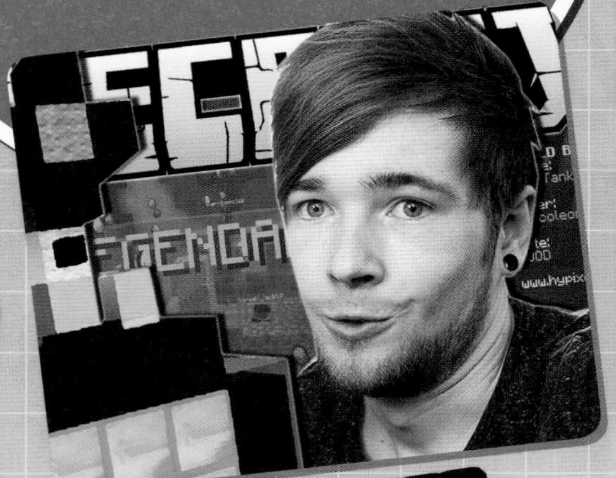

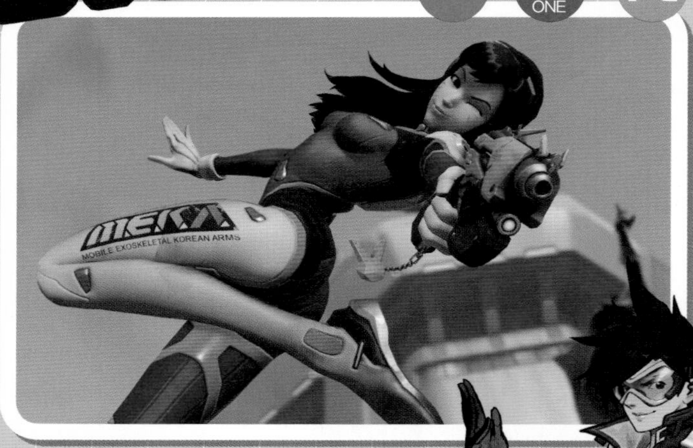

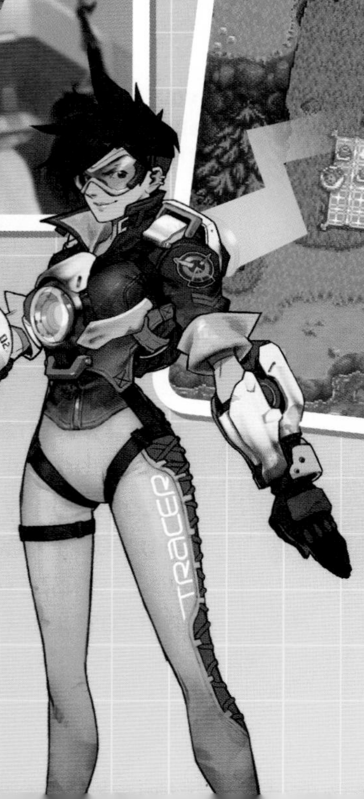

STARDEW VALLEY

PC

Grow your own way without getting dirt under your nails! An agricultural simulator might sound like hard work, but Stardew Valley is so smart and sweet that you'll want to give it all up and live on a farm.

Stardew Valley is one of 2016's prettiest games!

OVERWATCH

PS4 · XBOX ONE · PC

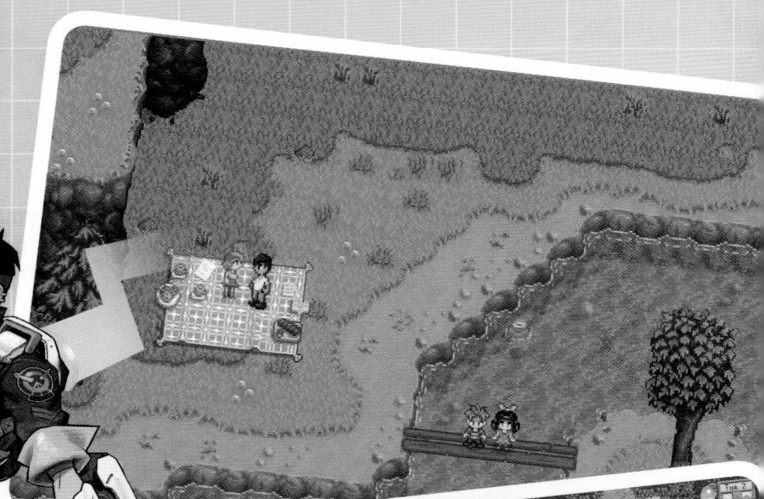

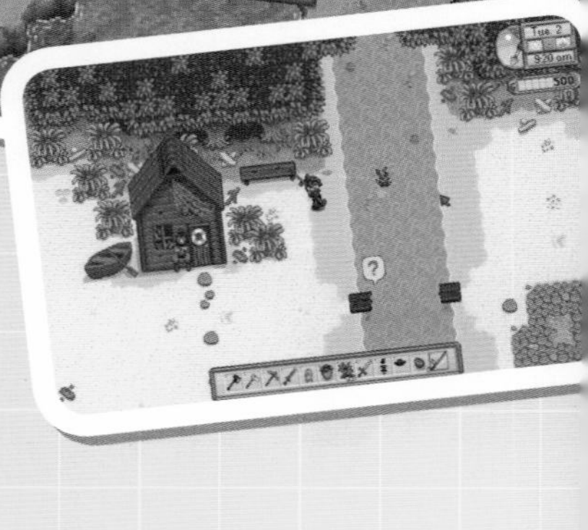

This one might be too shooty for some, but if you're old enough to play it (it's rated 12), it's flippin' brilliant. The cast of characters is *huge*, and includes giant scientist gorillas, hulking robots and deadly bounty hunters. And if you don't think Tracer (right) is cool, well, we probably can't be friends anymore.

RATCHET & CLANK

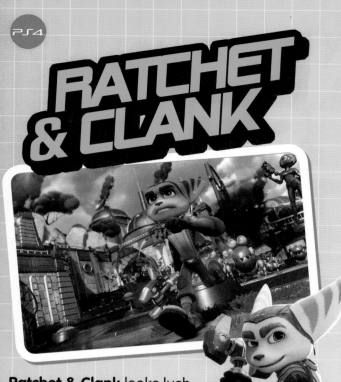

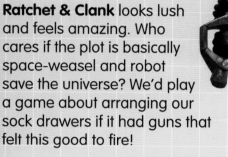

Ratchet & Clank looks lush and feels amazing. Who cares if the plot is basically space-weasel and robot save the universe? We'd play a game about arranging our sock drawers if it had guns that felt this good to fire!

MINECRAFT

Yeah, it's not exactly *new* – but imagine what you could build in six weeks. Castles! Moats! Castles with moats! The mind boggles. There's also a recent update to play with, so if you haven't crafted any mines for a while, now's the time to dive back in.

YO-KAI WATCH

This one is ideal if you want something that *feels* like you're playing outside when you're actually stuck indoors. Explore the undergrowth, hunt hidden monsters with your magic watch, then make 'em fight! It's better than collecting actual, icky bugs, right?

Now we want a magic watch too!

ROCKET LEAGUE

Like Minecraft it's not new, but still amazing. It's no longer just about cars and football, either – there are hockey and basketball modes, too! Even so, you still can't beat the brilliant, gormless bounce of the ball and the feeling of smashing home the perfect goal!

TEN EXCUSES TO KEEP PLAYING MINECRAFT

We've all been there. You're just putting the finishing touches on your majestic castle when your mum/dad/teacher nags you to stop playing Minecraft, for silly reasons like 'eating' and 'sleeping' and 'homework'. Next time it happens, use one of these excuses!

1 I'M LEARNING WHILE I'M PLAYING – COME ON, THIS IS PRACTICALLY HOMEWORK!
MolCraft – a downloadable Minecraft world – teaches you all about chemistry. Learn about molecules as you play – it's educational, y'see!

2 I CAN'T STOP NOW, I'M ON THE VERGE OF A SCIENTIFIC BREAKTHROUGH!
qCraft is a free mod that introduces quantum physics to your game – start playing with this on, and you'll be a genius by the time you're grown up.

3 **IF I STOP PLAYING MINECRAFT, CAN I WATCH A MOVIE INSTEAD?**
Not just any movie – the original Star Wars remade in Minecraft! No sound, but you can hum the music and do your own voices. Bet you do a mean Chewbacca…

4 **GO TO THE THEATRE? BUT WITH MINECRAFT, I'M ALREADY THERE!**
Show anti-gaming parents this excellent recreation of the Globe Theatre – the stomping ground of that William Shakespeare dude. No parent could accuse you of mindless gaming when you're learning about the Bard.

5 **MINECRAFT IS TEACHING ME TO COMPUTER CODE. LEAVE ME ALONE, OR I'LL BLOCK YOU FROM THE INTERNET FOREVER**
We all use computers, but how do our favourite apps and games work? Download LearnToMod and you can play Minecraft and learn to code at the same time.

6 GO TO AN ART GALLERY? FOOLISH PARENTS, MINECRAFT LETS ME LIVE IN ART

Ever dreamed of climbing inside your favourite paintings and having a wander about? Tate Worlds is a series of free maps wherein you can explore worlds based on famous art.

7 NO I CAN'T PLAY OUTSIDE, I'M TRAVELLING THE WORLD

This is no idle get out. Take a stroll through several Minecraft mods and you could tick off the entire Seven Wonders Of The World by lunchtime. Mount Rushmore, the Eiffel Tower, all of Denmark – just a few mouse clicks away.

8 I'M NOT PLAYING A GAME, I'M TRAINING TO BECOME A TOWN PLANNER

A staff member of the City of Ottawa took the city's open data and created GeoOttaWOW – giving users access to faithful recreations of roads, streets and landmarks of Canada's capital. They hope it will inspire kids to develop an interest in city planning. That's what our giant zombie pit is – the future of Canadian infrastructure.

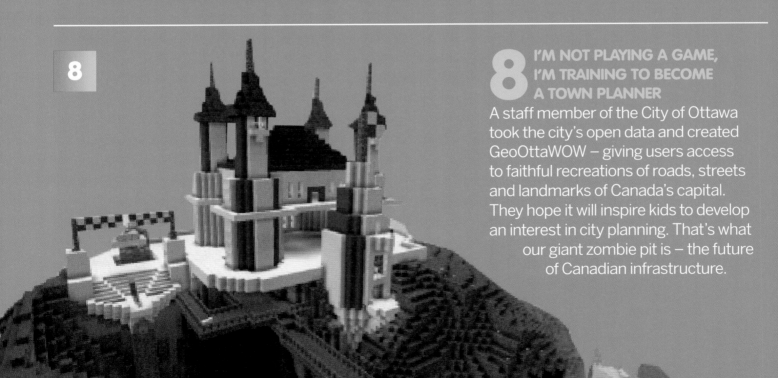

Iron Pickaxe

9 I WASN'T PLAYING MINECRAFT, I WAS CRAFTING THE ULTIMATE ROMANTIC GESTURE

Show your special someone that you love them nearly as much as Minecraft with this heartwarming 'I LUV U' message. If they ask why you sculpted it from dirt, laugh in their face (romantically) and explain that you need the diamonds for more important crafting projects. Get rejected, and you get more alone time with Minecraft. That's a win-win!

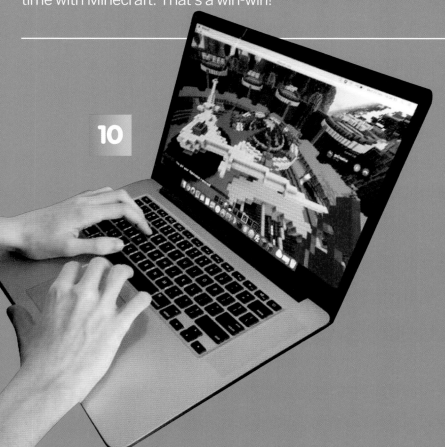

10 'PLAYING' MINECRAFT? HOW DARE YOU! I'M MAKING US RICH

Brandon Relph, 15, owns a business helping clients build whatever they want created in Minecraft. He's already made over £10,000. So get your mum and dad off your back by explaining you're on the verge of the next million dollar Minecraft idea. Maybe they'll invest too?

CaptainSparklez

Real Name: Jordan Maron
Channel: www.youtube.com/c/captainsparklez
Famous for... His amazing music and animations.

⦿ INSTAGRAM

Jordan celebrates killing 'a bunch of Horde Scum' in Warcraft!

Bad news - Sparklez and pals managed to crash their sick yacht!

'Don't you wish your cheekbones were hot like me?' asks Jordan!

FAVOURITE GAME

Trials Fusion

Who doesn't like dirt bikes and extreme stunts?! One of the best bits of this racer is making your own courses and games. No wonder Jordan loves it!

VITAL STATS

Channel start date:
20th July 2010
Subscriber count:
9,269,535
Most watched video:
Revenge

WRECKED AND A HALF!

1 Minecraft Style
"Dig, dig, dig, dig..."
This hilarious take on Gangnam Style makes us want to blockily dance along.

2 Star Wars Adventure
CaptainSparklez becomes one with the Force as he takes attempts to take down AT-ATs.

OUR FAVE

3 Revenge
It's four years old now, but this song is still so catchy – plus we can all relate to wanting some revenge on Creepers.

MAKE IT!
GROW YOUR OWN GRASS BLOCK!!!

Fancy making your own Minecraft grass block? Of course you do. And it's really pretty simple with our five step guide.

YOU'LL NEED...

MATERIALS: Square flower pot; grass/cress/chive seeds, or a small plant (we used a chive plant); green and brown foam; felt-tip pens; scissors; double-sided sticky tape; ruler and pen

RULER

BROWN FOAM

STICKY TAPE

GRASS, CRESS OR CHIVE SEEDS!

PENS!

GREEN FOAM

THE HUMBLE GRASS BLOCK CAN BE YOURS TO LOVE IN REAL LIFE!

GROW A GRASS BLOCK!

INFO

DIFFICULTY: EASY
TIME NEEDED: 20 MINUTES
TELL MUM?: YES. YOU MAY NEED HELP WITH SCISSORS

1 MEASURE UP

Use a ruler to measure the width of your flowerpot
Add about half a centimetre to the overall measurement, in order to give space for the corners. Then, using a ruler, carefully measure out four panes of this width on the brown foam. It's also a good idea to leave a flap of a centimetre or two at one end.

USE YOUR RULER TO MEASURE YOUR FLOWERPOT

2 FOLD IT UP

Carefully cut out your sheet of brown foam, keeping the edges as straight as possible. Line up the ruler along each fold line, and use your scissors to score it - this will help you to make each fold as sharp as possible. Turn the foam over, and use a brown felt-tip to decorate the 'earth' section of your block.

MAKE IT LOOK NICE AND EARTHY WITH YOUR PEN. IT'S A DIRTY JOB!

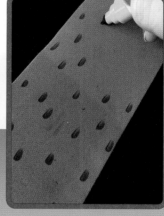

3 LOOK SHARP!

Turn the foam back over so that it's sat decoration-side down, and fold along your scored lines. Make sure you're folding them so that the decoration sits on the outside. If you're not used to using sharp scissors, get some help from an adult. We don't want any accidents!

GET AN ADULT TO HELP YOU WITH THE SCISSORS

4 IN A FLAP...

Attach pieces of double-sided sticky tape to the reverse side of each pane, and then carefully stick it to your flowerpot, lining it up with the bottom edge. Start off with the small flap, so that it can be covered by the final pane.

5 TA-DA!

Repeat steps 1-4 using green foam, but this time with much smaller panes and using green felt-tip pens. Cut small notches along the bottom, attach with tape, then finally, fill your pot!

Pokémon SUN

3DS

Pokémon MOON

Everything you need to know about the new Pokémon games!

Choose Rowlet, Litten or Popplio!

WHAT'S NEW?

We already knew that there was a new Pokémon game on the way for the Nintendo 3DS this year, but now we've finally got a good look at it, with lots of juicy new details. You set off adventuring on a Tropical Island called Alola where you can collect and battle monsters called Pokémon. You'll fight trainers and gym leaders in the game along the way, but you'll also be able to trade Pokémon with your friends or fight them to prove who's best. You begin by picking your first Pokémon from grass-type Rowlet, fire-type Litten, and water-type Popplio, and then battling your way to becoming the Pokémon champion. It's out in late November, so if you're reading this before Christmas, get in on your list for Santa!

ROWLET

This little owl is a grass *and* flying type Pokemon that can turn his head all the way back to look at his trainer during battle. We like his little bow tie and he has already become a firm favourite of Pokémon fans on the internet.

LEGENDARY

There are two versions of the game, each with a legendary Pokémon on the front. If you choose the Sun version you'll find a fiery-looking lion called Solgaleo, and if you pick Moon you'll find a huge mystical bird called Lunala. Which one will you go for?

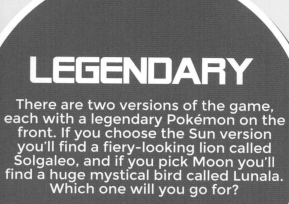

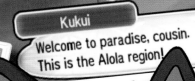

Kukui
Welcome to paradise, cousin. This is the Alola region!

I'm cute, but not as cute as Rowlet!

LITTEN

This fire type licks its flammable fur so it can attack by spitting up fiery hairballs. Why can't it just use normal, non-hairy flames like everyone else?!

POPPLIO

Part sea-lion, part clown, this water type can create huge bubbles to bounce off or trap other Pokémon in. Maybe it learnt to do that at the circus...

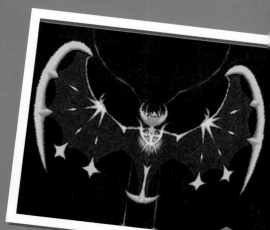

QUIZ!

1. Stampy's cat loves the camera, but can you remember its name?

2. What game does Bajan Canadian love playing other than Minecraft?

3. What Pokémon-style nickname did Dan TDM once give his pug Darcie?

4. Which pop star does iHasCupquake look like in an Instagram pic?

5. CaptainSparklez' favourite game is a racer, but what's its name?

6. What is the real-life name of the super-lovely iHasCupquake?

7. What gets eaten a lot in Stampy's Minecraft video School Days?

8. Which animal did Bajan Canadian hang out with in Australia?

9. What's the name of the CaptainSparklez vid with 162 million views?

10. Which character does Dan TDM meet in his most popular video?

ANSWERS

1 Ori
2 League Of Angels
3 Pika-Pug
4 Lady Gaga
5 Trials Fusion
6 Tiffany Herrera
7 Cookies
8 Kangaroo
9 Revenge
10 Dr Trayaurus

Dan TDM

Real Name: Dan Middleton
Channel: youtube.com/user/TheDiamondMinecart
Famous for... His great Minecraft video series and stories, as well as all of his invented characters.

INSTAGRAM

Dressing his dog Darcie up as a unicorn. Don't try this at home!

Teeth for eyes? We are totally freaked out right now!

Darcie gets given a temporary new name in this outfit: Pika-Pug!

FAVOURITE GAME

Minecraft

Because of course it is – it's the game that made him famous, and we do love watching him playing it while inventing new characters.

VITAL STATS

Channel start date:
14 July 2012
Subscriber count:
10,947,412
Most watched video:
How I met Dr Trayaurus

C'MERE YOU LIL' PUNK!

BEST VIDS

1 Fat Pikachu
Dan and friends take on a Pokémon-themed build challenge and come across a *huge* Pikachu.

2 Biggest Dance Party Ever
An epic game of Block Party turns into a dance off as they run around to avoid falling.

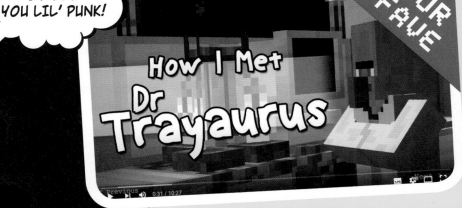

OUR FAVE

How I Met Dr Trayaurus

3 How I Met Dr Trayaurus
It's Dan's most watched vid for a reason! Who knew a simple house move could lead to such a wonderful, lasting friendship?!

WHAT'S NEW?

The best thing about new Lego Star Wars isn't just reliving the movie – you also get to play stories that weren't in the film. If you know your Star Wars you'll be aware that The Force Awakens picks up where Return Of The Jedi left off (all the way back in 1983!), and the new Lego game lets you play all the exciting stuff that happened in between. There are seven new tales in total, including how C-3PO got his mysterious red hand, Poe Dameron's brave rescue of Admiral Ackbar, and Han Solo and Chewbacca's mission to capture the Rathtars. Plus you can control more than 200 characters (with even more, like Jabba The Hutt, coming as DLC) and fly the Millennium Falcon! The Force is incredibly strong with this one.

Collect studs as Rey, Finn, BB-8 and all your Force Awakens favourites!

RATHTAR
Bad news: Chewie's gonna get ya!

REY
Even more attitude than Princess Leia

BB-8
Our new Star Wars fave – sorry R2-D2!

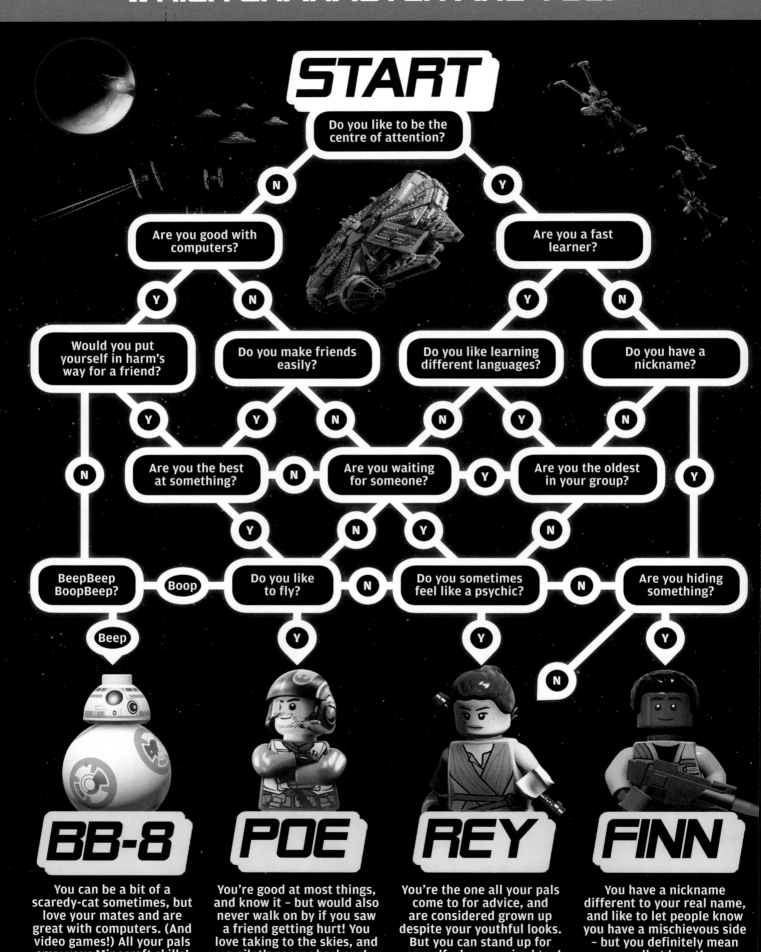

START

Do you like to be the centre of attention?

N — Are you good with computers?

Y — Are you a fast learner?

Y — Would you put yourself in harm's way for a friend?

N — Do you make friends easily?

Y — Do you like learning different languages?

N — Do you have a nickname?

Are you the best at something?

Are you waiting for someone?

Are you the oldest in your group?

BeepBeep BoopBeep? — Boop — Do you like to fly? — N — Do you sometimes feel like a psychic? — N — Are you hiding something?

Beep

Y

Y

Y

N

BB-8
You can be a bit of a scaredy-cat sometimes, but love your mates and are great with computers. (And video games!) All your pals envy your Minecraft skills!

POE
You're good at most things, and know it – but would also never walk on by if you saw a friend getting hurt! You love taking to the skies, and a pilot's career beckons!

REY
You're the one all your pals come to for advice, and are considered grown up despite your youthful looks. But you can stand up for yourself when required too!

FINN
You have a nickname different to your real name, and like to let people know you have a mischievous side – but you definitely mean well at heart!

A

B

C

D

E

F

G

?
GUESS WHO...

It's Pokémon mania –
you gotta name 'em all!

THE CAT'S WHISKERS

Get to know the YouTube superstar better with our smashing Stampy special

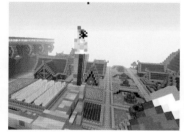

Chances are, if you're reading this gloriously chunky gaming annual, you know just who Stampy is. You've watched his videos, shared his adventures, perhaps even bought his lovely book. But for anyone who doesn't play Minecraft, he's a bit of a mystery. Many folk could easily stroll past Stampy in the street, unaware they almost rubbed shoulders with a YouTube superstar; a man who gets more YouTube hits than many successful pop stars, with

a legion of dedicated, block-bashing followers. Many mainstream newspapers and websites run bemused stories, struggling to understand why we tune in to watch hours of pretend things being built in a virtual world. Of course, anyone who's watched Stampy's videos - or played Minecraft themselves - will know why.

That's why the next few pages are dedicated to Stampy, whose real name is Joseph Garrett. We were lucky enough to interview him, and naturally we asked him for all his closely guarded YouTube secrets: they might not be enough to propel us to internet

superstardom, but his top ten tips are still a smashing place to start. Whether it's YouTube tips, Stampy's favourite Minecraft block or his proudest achievements, we've got you covered. On top of that, we've also got a list of essential Stampy facts that everyone should know - some familiar, others less so. If you're already a fan, slice yourself a whopping great piece of cake, sit back and enjoy; if not, hopefully we can convince you to give Stampy's lovely channel a look.

STAMPY FACTS

He's one of YouTube's biggest stars, but how much do we really know about Stampy? Well, rather a lot, actually. Below is a list of some fascinating Stampy tidbits, including his rise to stardom, spin-off channels and motivation. For ease, we refer to Stampy and Joseph as the same person - it can get confusing with all those names!

01 Stampy's channel is one of the fastest growing channels of any genre. He currently averages around 3,500 new subscribers every single day - more than enough to fill Wembley Stadium every month.

02 His daily views are pretty darn impressive, too. His videos average over four million daily views - that's way more than the entire population of Berlin, or all of Georgia, in a single day!

Is this a gigantic Stampy statue, or just perspective?

STAMPY SPEAKS OUT

Inspiration, advice and tasty Minecraft tips from the YouTube superstar

You don't become a YouTube success overnight. As well as years of hard work, epic levels of dedication and a charming demeanour, you also need to be really rather good at your game of choice. With this in mind, we recently got the chance to chat to Stampy

about his greatest successes, inspiration and the secret to succeeding at YouTube.

We also dig in to more technical stuff, such as why Minecraft is such a great fit for YouTube videos. We're a bit greedy, so we also asked him for his top ten tips for Minecraft success. And because he's a

thoroughly decent sort, he was kind enough to oblige us. Stampy's tips are ideal for refining your game or preparing you for a lucrative career as a Minecrafting YouTube superstar. Heed his advice, and remember your ol' friends if you ever become billionaires...

03 Stampy uploads new videos every day, which can often take many hours to make and upload. It might look like the best job in the world, but it's still really hard work.

04 In December 2013, Stampy's channel was temporarily terminated by Google. After petitions, outrage, and the #SaveStampy hashtag trending on Twitter, Google apologised and reinstated his channel. To this day, we don't know why it was terminated.

05 Stampy didn't start off making Minecraft videos. Instead, he recorded amusing real-life skits, as well as stop-motion animation. The name Stampylonghead comes from one of these animations.

06 Joseph studied video production at college and university. As uni work began to take up loads of his time, he set up the Stampylonghead channel to upload less time-consuming Let's Play videos. The rest is YouTube history.

07 His first gaming videos weren't all about Minecraft, either. He started off recording commentaries over games such as Call of Duty and Halo. His first foray into Minecraft was on the Xbox 360 version.

Can you remember your first experience of Minecraft? What was it exactly that got you hooked?
My first experience with Minecraft was my first episode in My Lovely World. It is a long running series that I still do to this day. The complete freedom and possibilities were what got me hooked.

What is it about Minecraft - and specifically, your Minecraft videos - that inspires and engages so many people?
I think people enjoy the humour and stories that I tell in my videos. They also come as a source of inspiration when they might not be sure what they want to build.

Minecraft has an active and engaged community, perhaps more so than any other game. Why do you think this is?
I think the Minecraft audience has stayed engaged for so long because there is always something new to do in the game. The community and developers are always adding something new.

Why is YouTube so important for Minecraft?
YouTube is so important to Minecraft because for many it is where they first hear about Minecraft. It is the most popular video game on YouTube and helps to spread the word about the game. I think it also encourages people to continue to

"I THINK PEOPLE MAINLY ENJOY THE HUMOUR AND STORIES I TELL IN MY VIDEOS"

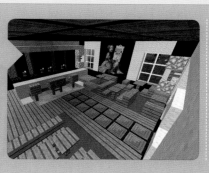

08 Before becoming a YouTube hit, Joseph was a barman. He left his job to focus solely on videos when he started earning enough to do it for a living. At the time, he was on 10,000 subscribers, rather than the *seven million* he's approaching now.

09 He's doing amazingly well now, but his beginnings were reassuringly humble: Joseph started out filming in his bedroom at his parents' house.

10 Joseph met his buddy iBallisticSquid in January 2013. They became fast friends and YouTube collaborators, and have a joint channel called The Magic Animal Club.

11 In a display of parental awesomeness, Joseph's parents were happy for him to live rent-free until he could develop his channel into a full time career. Thanks, Mr & Mrs Garrett!

"IT'S A LOT MORE FUN TO PUT ALL YOUR ENERGY INTO MAKING GREAT VIDEOS."

play because they want to replicate what they see in videos.

What's the most difficult thing you've ever built?
The most difficult thing I have built is a working treadmill. I also spent a lot of time building a giant frog that I am rather proud of.

What's your proudest Minecraft achievement?
My proudest Minecraft achievement is My Lovely World. I have been building it for so long, and I am proud that I am able to continue coming up with ideas for new things to add.

If you could give your fans one piece of advice about becoming a YouTuber, what would it be?
My advice for being a YouTuber is to focus on the videos and not YouTube. It is easy to get overwhelmed with YouTube stats and trying to get views. It's a lot more fun to put all of your energy just into making great videos.

You're obviously a huge gamer, and your videos aren't just about Minecraft. Has the games industry changed since you started doing this?
The gaming industry has changed in so many ways since I have started. YouTube (and YouTubers) have really started having an impact on the success of games. You can see many more games targeted directly at YouTubers in the hope that they will play the game. The rise of free to play and mobile games is also having dramatic effects on the entire industry.

How did you come up with the name 'Stampy Longhead'?
It was originally the name of a character in an animation I made at school.

How long does it take you to make each of your videos in total?
Some series I can record several videos in one day. Bigger videos can take over a week of work on just one video. 95% of what I do is planning.

What is your favourite Minecraft block and why?
My favourite block to build out of is sandstone because not many people use it and I love the texture and colour. It also reminds me of white chocolate.

What's been your favourite quest in Minecraft?
My favourite quest in My Lovely World was probably in the episode "Cat to the Future". I make the world's tastiest cake and go back in time so I can eat it more than once. I accidently go back too far and end up in an epic adventure. ∎

12 Want more awesome parenting? The logo on Joseph's channel, featuring Mr Stampy Cat, was designed by his father, and his mum helps run his Facebook page.

13 Stampy's audience is largely comprised of six to 14-year-olds, and the majority of them are girls. Even then, it's a pretty even 60/40 split, proving, if it were even necessary, that Minecraft is for everyone.

14 Stampy gets well over 3,000 messages a day - far more than he can physically answer. They're not just about Minecraft, either. Sometimes, his fans just tell him how their day went!

15 Want to understand how big Stampy is? Well, in 2014, he had the fourth biggest channel on YouTube - wedged between pop gigastars Katy Perry and Shakira. Lovely!

The quest for tasty cake takes Stampy to spooky places

16 Because Stampy's videos are aimed at a specific audience, he makes sure it's all family friendly. You won't find any swearing, and the emphasis is on good, clean, creative fun.

17 Stampy now has a second channel, called Wonder Quest. It features a 12-episode show of the same name. It's still made in Minecraft, but the production values are snazzier, and it's more educational. Wonderful!

18 Wonder Quest draws on Joseph's previous experience in video production. It's completely scripted - rather than the spontaneous stuff in his other shows - and even features original music and sound effects.

19 Every episode of Wonder Quest has an educational angle. In order to overcome a particular challenge, Stampy usually has to learn something new. Suddenly, the name makes a lot of sense!

20 The spin-off channel also features the I Wonder cartoon series - more traditional animation that digs deeper into the educational themes of Wonder Quest. Thankfully, entertainment is still the most important aspect.

TOP 10 TIPS FROM STAMPY

Polish your Minecraft skills with Stampy's handy tips

1 Sleep tight. On your first night make sure your number one priority is to make a bed. You don't want to be caught outside in the dark when the googlies spawn. Make a bed and sleep as soon as it starts to get dark.

2 Make sure you always use the right tool for the job. Start by making a wooden pickaxe so you can gather cobblestone, then make a set of stone tools. Once you have iron you can upgrade. Make sure you use an iron pickaxe to mine diamonds. Using the wrong tool to destroy a block is slow and will eventually destroy the tool.

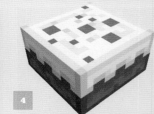

3 Don't get lost. Create a map and make a note of where your house is. When exploring a cave leave a trail of torches behind you so you can follow them to get back out. Do the same when exploring the Nether. You can also look at the sun or moon to work out which way is North. When in a cave you can check the texture of cobblestone to find out which way is North.

4 Don't go hungry. One of the first things you should do in a new world is get a good supply of food. The easiest way to get food at first is meat. Once you have a house, making a wheat farm should be a top priority. Eventually you can also plant carrots and potatoes. If you want something tastier then make a cake!

5 Protect your house from googlies. Keeping the area around your house bright is very important. The googlies only spawn when it's dark. You could also dig a pit around your base that the googlies can't jump over. Setting up traps can also be helpful, just be careful not to get caught in them yourself.

---

21 Stampy's collaborators in Wonder Quest include CaptainSparklez, AmyLee33, EvanTubeHD, ShayCarl, and his real-life buddy iBallisticSquid - all Minecraft superstars in their own right.

22 Wonder Quest has been a huge success. The channel has more than 45 million views, and a second series is on the way. I Wonder has even been used as an educational tool in some schools.

23 Stampy isn't just huge on YouTube, either - he has over 400 thousand followers on Twitter and nearly 700 thousand likes on Facebook. Give us a retweet, Stampy!

24 Stampy's first video was published in May 2012, but the tone is slightly different from the one we know and love today - instead, his early videos are more like direct, traditional game reviews.

25 Stampy deliberately keeps his personal life separate from his YouTube videos. This is partly because Minecraft is more fun, but also because he considers himself a video producer, not a vlogger.

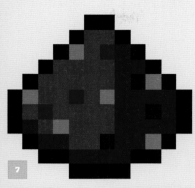

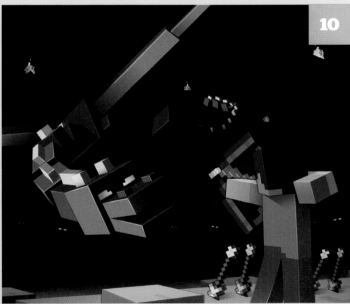

6 Get diamonds. Diamonds are probably the most precious and useful item in the game. To find them you need to dig right down to the bottom of the world. It is much easier to find them when in a natural cave but is safer to find them when digging in a straight line. When you find diamonds it's best to go home or put them in a chest to make sure they stay safe.

7 **Learn redstone. Lots of people are scared to try and learn how redstone works but it can be really useful. Try experimenting with it to see what it can do. Try making a doorbell or use pistons to make a secret doorway. It can also make very useful things that make your life much easier.**

8 Get creative. You can get bored of playing Minecraft if you don't have an idea for something to build. If you don't know what to build try building your house or school. Building giant versions of your favourite characters is fun too. If you still don't know what to build try watching one of my videos and try re-building what I build but do it in your own style.

9 **Play with friends. Minecraft can get lonely when playing by yourself. Inviting friends can make it lots more fun. Work on a project together or compete against each other in challenges. If you are on PC you can go on a server and play with 1000s of people. Just be careful to only talk to people that you know in real life.**

10 Defeat the dragon. Defeating the Ender Dragon is one of the toughest challenges in Minecraft. Before entering The End make sure you are 100% prepared for the battle. Bring lots of food and equipment. You want at least a full set of iron armour but diamond would be better. You want a bow and LOTS of arrows. Putting a pumpkin on your head means that the Endermen won't attack you unless you attack them first. You also want to bring blocks that can be used to pile up.

STAMPY'S
LOVELY BOOK

Lovely puzzles, games, comic strips, video tips, secrets and ____!

26 Joseph has also appeared on mainstream TV. As well as doing interviews, he was a judge on the CBBC series Appsolute Genius - part of the BBC's Make it Digital initiative, aimed at inspiring a new generation of coders.

27 Joseph's videos are made using the console version of Minecraft, but he'd like to see more parity between platforms - things like cross-platform play and shareable levels.

28 Despite being a superstar, Joseph isn't a massive fan of crowds: thankfully, he's okay being on stage in front of his legions of viewers, though (not to mention the millions watching at home).

29 Stampy was friends with most of his YouTube collaborators before he became famous - they're people who knew each other in real life, and got into YouTube together, which is exactly why his collaborations work so well.

30 Despite being based in a sleepy part of England, Stampy is an international success: 50% of his viewers are based in the US, and 25% are from the UK.

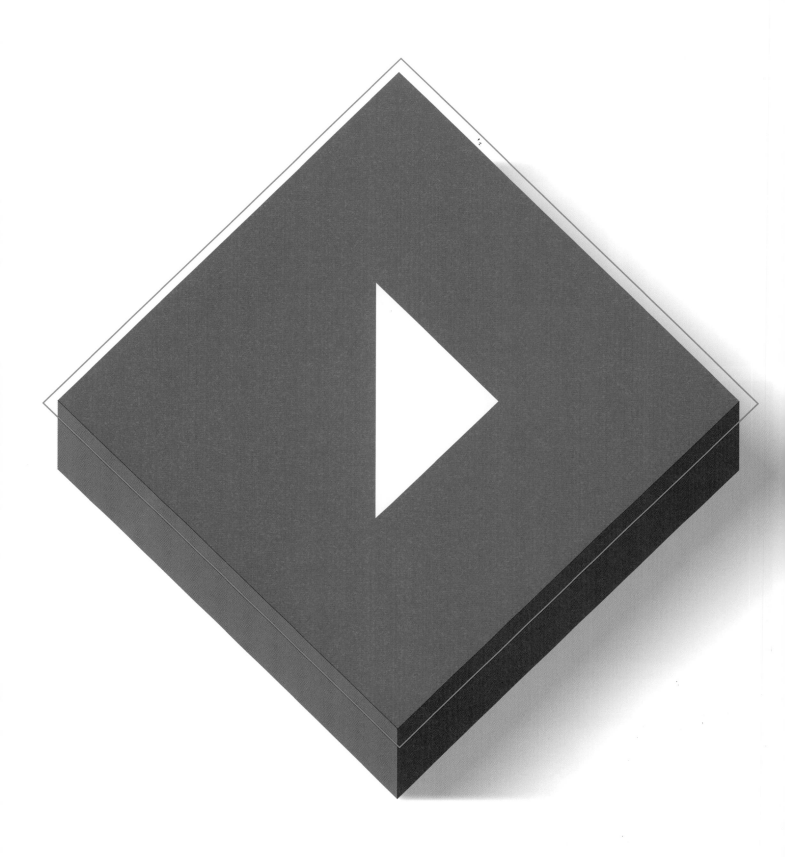

LET'S PLAY!

Meet the YouTube legends who share their in-game adventures with the world.

It's hard to overstate the popularity of Minecraft on YouTube. The video-sharing platform is a home to tens of thousands of gamers who upload their escapades to be enjoyed by a wider community. At the moment, those videos have been viewed more than 32 billion times. Wowsers!

As with any community, there are superstars who've gathered a huge audience. They have hundreds of thousands of fans, and with the money they earn from their channel, a lucky few are even able to quit their jobs and play Minecraft for a living.

If you want to join those hallowed ranks, we've gathered together some advice for you from the very best. Over the next few pages, you'll learn from Minecraft superstars about the tricks needed to create a brilliant Minecraft channel. Just don't forget us when you're raking in the cash...

YOUTUBER
INTERVIEW

Mumbo Jumbo

We sit and chat with Redstone expert and rising YouTube star Mumbo Jumbo. Join us as we natter about Minecraft in schools, the basics of circuitry, and how YouTube made Mojang's finest what it is today...

PROFILE

Alias MumboJumbo

Channel
www.youtube.com/user/
ThatMumboJumbo

Expertise
Building with Redstone

Most viewed video
www.youtube.com/
watch?v=1CAp2NmhZEU

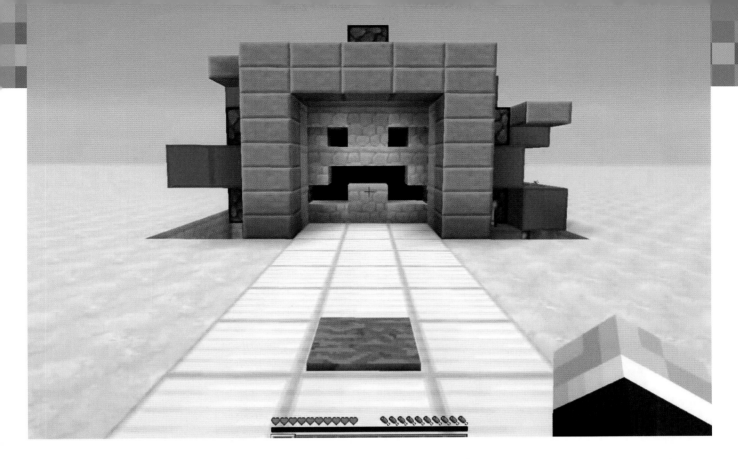

Going back, can you remember your first experience of Minecraft, and can you tell us what it was like?

I remember it because some people at my school were talking about Minecraft and they were chatting about this game and saying it looks like Lego. You know what: I quite like Lego! So I hopped onto the computer. I asked my mum's permission to buy it, because I was a little bit younger at the time. I got it and I was up till about 4am working on my first hut. It was made entirely out of dirt. It had holes in the roof for the torches and I remember on the first night I tried to sleep and just immediately got blown up. That was one of my first experiences of Minecraft. I'm glad I kept it up, but that could have been the end, almost!

Did you have any idea then how big the game would eventually become?

Oh, no, definitely not. I got it in the Alpha stage. Back then you'd tell people: 'I play Minecraft' and they'd be confused. They'd be like: 'the graphics are awful!' They'd talk about how terrible it looked compared to all the other games…

What makes Minecraft such an enticing prospect for you?

It's just raw creativity. You make the fun in the game. It's not like Call Of Duty or something like that. You have a very defined role in Call Of Duty where you have to go along and kill the other team. It's great fun, but as far as Minecraft is concerned, there are no real instructions. There's no real goal or

motive. I mean technically you don't have to do *anything* in the game. You can just walk around and punch trees! But you make your own little journey. It's great fun messing around with what's possible in this world, like I do with redstone, to see what I can do there.

There are plenty of possibilities, for example, in building and things. You can build a giant castle. Nobody needs to build a giant castle! It's not one of the aims of the game at all, but it's just one of those things you can do if you want to.

The castle is pretty much the go to for everyone, right? Funny that!

Yeah!

Do you think Minecraft should be held up as an educational resource for younger kids?

I guess so, yes. It requires quite a lot of

logical thought and it forces you to be a lot more creative than other things in the market. If people are getting into redstone, it teaches you some of the fundamental things about Boolean logic, which is to say the fundamentals of computing. That's a pretty big deal. Outside of that, it forces you to be creative and use your brain and assess what you're doing and better whatever it is that you're working on.

And then there's the community aspect as well. Are you proud to be a member of the wider Minecraft community?

It's one of the more friendly communities I can think of on the internet. It was extremely welcoming. When I started out on YouTube, everyone who's a similar size to you will help you out. Everyone seems to have a common

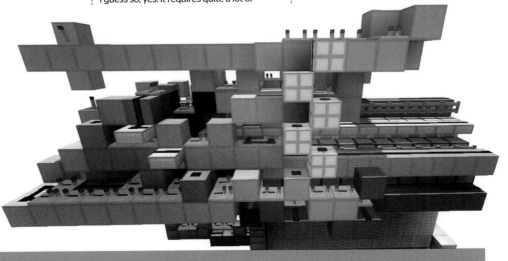

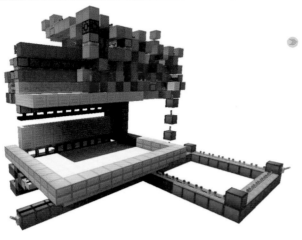

interest in Minecraft, and obviously you get involved in your own little communities. If you're all working together, as a team, it allows you to build friendships quite easily. There are plenty of little servers that are people from all over the world working together as a little group on their various projects and things. I've experienced that, and it's something you see right the way throughout the community.

What makes Minecraft perfect for crafting videos around?
It comes back to the fact that the person who's creating the video has full control

over the content they're producing. In other games it relies on being extremely good at one aspect. Here you can just have fun with friends on a server, and that will make a good video because you're clearly having fun! Other than that there's the whole tutorial aspect. You can show people various bits, how to do the technical elements, and also you have the full Let's Play. It's essentially limitless. There's not a set achievement structure. Let's Plays can run on for hundreds of episodes without running out of content. That's one of the main things that's kept it going so well in terms of YouTube. Obviously you have the whole modding side, there's always content available.

TOP TIPS

Worried you'll never get those pistons working? Let Mumbo Jumbo set you up with some essential starter tips.

1
THINK LOGICALLY

"My first tip, which is something I did right at the very beginning, was that I made sure I thought everything through logically before building. There's nothing worse than getting everything set up thinking that you're going to have it all working, and then looking at the giant mess you've created, and thinking: 'I'm lost!' Think it through logically and try to think how the redstone circuits are going to function."

2
USE COLOURED WOOL

"A really handy thing to do is to make your redstone circuitry with coloured wool. That will allow you to have different colours for different circuits for different things. This will really help you out. It allows you to segregate what does what, and enables you to troubleshoot in your own circuits."

How important is YouTube for Minecraft?
It's very important because without it I don't think Minecraft would be where it is today. That's my own personal opinion. The reason a lot of my friends found out about Minecraft is because some of the YouTubers that they were watching originally started playing Minecraft. They saw it and they thought… well first they thought it looked rubbish, but when they saw the creative elements and all the things that you could do with it they got into it. It's one of those games that blew up on YouTube pretty quickly, and suddenly it was in all of everyone's sub boxes and feeds, and people were looking into it and wondering 'what on earth *is* this thing?' That's the sort of thing that I don't think Minecraft could have achieved through traditional advertising. If you showed me an advert on the TV, and it was like: 'It's building. With blocks.' I'd just be like: 'that doesn't seem like anything I'd be interested in'. YouTube was a huge element for Minecraft's success.

"WITHOUT YOUTUBE I DON'T THINK MINECRAFT WOULD BE WHERE IT IS TODAY."

If you had the keys to YouTube is there anything you would change?
There'd be a few things in terms of the YouTube side of things. Like if they were a lot better at pushing videos to people that were subscribed to you. That seems to be something that YouTube are phasing out. It seems odd to me. That's the one thing I'd change. But it works as it is. It probably isn't perfect, but it does function well. And I'm yet to find myself looking for an alternative. Currently I'm perfectly happy on YouTube. It suits me down to the ground. A few little tiny problems, but other than that it's running smoothly.

And if you had the keys to Minecraft, what would you change there?
I think there would be a few little bits. It

wouldn't be the hardcore elements of the game. They work perfectly fine. But in terms of my own little niche of redstone, there are a few little elements I wouldn't mind adding. Cogs, pulleys, things like that. That would be really good fun and would add a whole new area of the world. Other than that, it's probably not perfect. There are plenty of bugs in Minecraft and there are things people like to complain about, but you forget that it's a game that functions perfectly well. I've played Minecraft for five years now. I paid 13 pounds for it, the best 13 pounds I've spent in my life. I'm in no position to complain!

What is your favourite build?
Aw blimey. This is going to be a tough one. I could take this a couple of routes. I could go for my first ever redstone contraption which was a 2x2 door that was using just wooden doors. That was one of my first ones so you could say it was one of my favourites. Phoar… I've… There's a lot of them. I don't know why but I've got a fond memory of the armour stand jump scare device. It's funny because it's so very pointless. It was when flying

blocks were first introduced, and we had the ability to launch entities at great speed. So I placed an armour stand behind the door and a flying block behind the armour stand. If you walked past it would just launch out at you, and I've always liked that contraption just because it was very silly.

What's the hardest thing you've ever had to do with redstone?
I'd almost go back to my first redstone project again! Oh, I don't know. I've worked on some things that have never come together, and I've worked on them for hours and hours on end. I know I say don't give up, but, when things go *so* wrong, you have to know when to stop! Looking back, they're getting on, but there was an infinitely expandable 5x5 door. Back then it required a lot of piston action, that was getting on two-and-a-half, maybe three years ago. That was my first proper large scale redstone project. That took a lot of work! ■

3
PACE YOURSELF
"One of the big parts of redstone is just practice. You're not going to immediately get into it, and you're not going to build insane contraptions. Think about the scope of your project. How big is your redstone contraption going to be? For your first one, don't make it a 30x30 door with crazy piston mechanics. Start off small. You need to know where you're standing and follow some redstone tutorials. They'll give you the basics of where you're going."

4
DO A DRY RUN
"As far as starting a project is concerned – say it's a piston mechanism for instance – it's always good to not do any circuitry. Do a dry run with levers and just toggle all of the inputs. Use these levers the way that it will run with the circuitry, just testing out the mechanisms."

5
KEEP AT IT!
"If it doesn't work: don't give up! It's very easy to do that, but it requires perseverance. It gets very very frustrating. I work with redstone every day. It can get very frustrating if something isn't working properly. You've probably been working at it for so long you don't know what you're looking at any more! So just keep at it! Take an hour break! Go away and watch some TV, come back and you never know, you might have the answer as soon as you come back to it. Once it's done, it's done. You can look at it and go: 'I built that! That's come out of my head!'"

YOUTUBER INTERVIEW

Aureylian

Infamous for breaking into song at any opportunity, Aureylian's YouTube videos have won her a legion of fans.

PROFILE

Alias Aureylian

Channel www.youtube.
com/user/Aureylian

Expertise
Minigames and Let's Play

Most viewed video
www.youtube.com/
watch?v=EJQMVFhYJGE

TOP TIPS

How to set your videos apart from the crowd and build a fanbase of your own.

1
BE WHO YOU ARE

"Minecraft is awesome, but most of the time people are watching your videos for your personality, not for the game itself."

2
LEARN TO EDIT

"There are some lulls in Minecraft occasionally (mining for coal, amirite?), and to keep people entertained you'll want to edit only the most entertaining or educational parts into the video and lose the rest – even if that means cutting out a huge bulk of what you recorded."

How did you first discover Minecraft?
A friend of mine came back from a LAN and said: "Hey you should try this game – a lot of people were playing it last weekend." When I first looked at it, I really didn't understand the entire premise and wasn't really feeling the throwback look. But as soon as I gave it an honest go, I was pretty much hooked.

Where do the ideas for your videos usually come from?
Oh, man... A lot of the time, we're sitting around like: "Wouldn't it be fun if...", and that's where we come up with stuff. Recently, I started a High-Stakes Minecraft series with a few other YouTubers, and it came about

"WHAT MAKES ME UNIQUE IS THE UNIQUE COMMUNITY THAT WATCHES MY VIDEOS."

just because we asked: "How can we up the ante this time?" – and that evolved into pies in the face and Twitter profile takeovers. Other times I use resources other gamers use, like mini-game directories, to see what new stuff the community comes up with to highlight.

How much work goes into each video you make before you hit publish?
For me, it takes about four times the end video length to produce. So, if there's a 25 minute video, it's taken about an extra hour to prepare, edit, render, upload, and design the thumbnail. Obviously that varies, but playing the game is really only a small piece.

What do you think makes you different?
I'm very outspoken about the acceptance of others within the community who typically feel like they don't fit in. I've tried to make my channel a home for my viewers, where they can form friendships, embrace what makes them unique, and support charities and human rights causes, all while geeking out with whatever video games or nerd culture I happen to feature in that video. What makes me unique is the unique (and epic) community that watches my videos.

Who are some of your favourite lesser-known YouTubers?
It depends on your definition of lesser-known.

The majority of content I watch on YouTube aren't gaming videos at all – more lifestyle and fashion. So, perhaps lesser known to the gaming space, but still popular in their own right, a few of my faves are GigiGorgous, SuperMaryFace, Domics, and Grav3yardgirl.

What do you think makes Minecraft so much more popular than other games?
It's so open and never ending, both literally in game, and externally with the modifications that can be made. Between prebuilt adventure maps, texture packs, mods that add new content, multi-player, single-player, mini-game servers etc, there's absolutely no way anyone could say: "I've done everything there is to do in Minecraft". It's great for kids, adults, and pretty much anyone in the history of forever who has enjoyed a video game, since the options are limitless and it can be customised to entertain everyone.

Finally, if you could add one new feature to vanilla Minecraft, what would it be?
I get asked this ALL the time and I never feel like I have a good answer! If I HAD to absolutely choose one thing, I guess I'd say more farming/cooking options, since my favourite mods have been Pam's Harvestcraft and Agriculture, both of which add hundreds of new plants to grow, recipes to make, and new tools for the kitchen. ∎

3
THINK OUTSIDE THE BOX
"If you're wondering what is going to make people watch YOUR video instead of someone else's, it's usually because your commentary or play style are different than the other people out there. Experiment, and don't be afraid to deviate from what the big guys are doing."

4
KEEP UP
"There are always new minigames, or adventure maps, or updates, or mods that get added to the game. Adding new types of content to your videos not only helps keep people coming back to see what new stuff you've done, but it'll also help you stay interested in the game."

5
HAVE FUN
"It's really not entertaining to watch someone who doesn't seem like they enjoy the game. Most likely, if it's fun for you, it'll be fun for viewers."

COOL STUFF!

You NEED this in your life!

This ace Funko Pop! figure of Overwatch's Tracer is even cuter than the real thing!

This Legend Of Zelda backpack will keep all of your adventuring gear safe

Did you know you can get amiibos of all your favourite Animal Crossing characters?

MEGA FAN!

Cosplayer Keren Lin looks ready for battle in her Hyrule Warriors-style Zelda outfit – complete with sword. She's one princess who doesn't need rescuing! You can find more awesome photos on Keren's Facebook page.

SING ALONG!

Did you know someone made a musical of Mario? It's exactly as weird as it sounds, with all your favourites singing on stage – Luigi, Princess Peach, Bowser, and, er, Pikachu. How'd he get involved?!

Love Star Wars? Then this Finn flight jacket is definitely for you!

Finally, the perfect clothing for launching yourself out of a catapult!

Turns out Plants Vs Zombies' Yeti isn't so hard to find after all – hunt one down!

The Minecraft Treehouse Lego set is seriously huge, with over 700 bricks! Mad!